D1288764

Rails in the Isle of Wight

P. C. ALLEN AND A. B. MACLEOD

DAVID & CHARLES
Newton Abbot   London   North Pomfret (VT)

British Library Cataloguing in Publication Data

Allen, *Sir, Peter, 1905*
   Rails in the Isle of Wight. – 2nd ed.
   1. Railways – England – Isle of Wight – History
   I. Title   II. MacLeod, A.B.
   385′.09422′8   HE3019.18

   ISBN 0-7153-8701-4

First published 1967 by George Allen & Unwin Ltd.
This second edition published by David & Charles, 1986

Printed in Great Britain
by Redwood Burn Limited, Trowbridge, Wilts
for David & Charles Publishers plc
Brunel House   Newton Abbot   Devon

Published in the United States of America
by David & Charles Inc
North Pomfret   Vermont 05053   USA

Contents

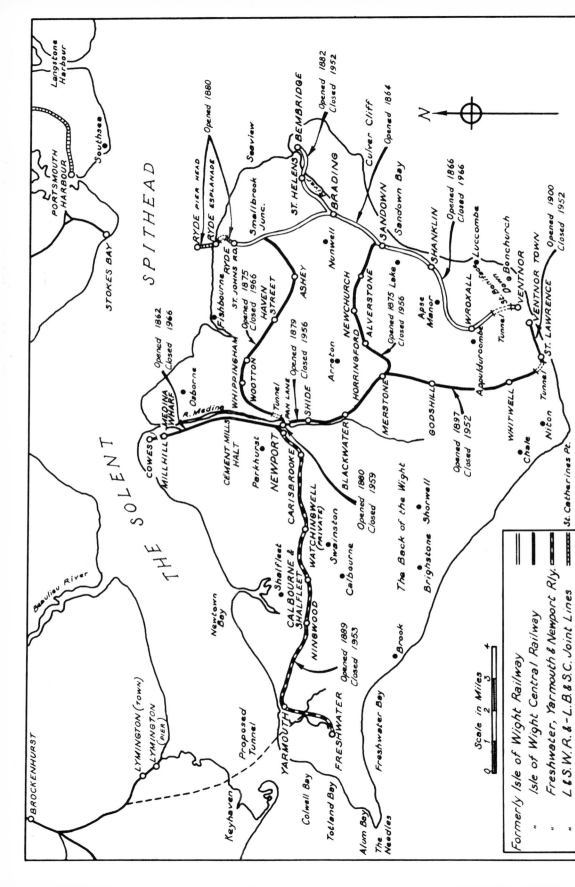

LANGSTONE HARBOUR

SOUTHSEA

PORTSMOUTH HARBOUR

STOKES BAY

SPITHEAD

Opened 1880

RYDE PIER HEAD
RYDE ESPLANADE
ST. JOHNS RD.
Smallbrook Junc.
Opened 1875 Closed 1966
RYDE
Fishbourne

Seaview
Smallbrook

Opened 1882 Closed 1952
BEMBRIDGE
ST. HELENS
BRADING
Culver Cliff

Opened 1864
SANDOWN
Sandown Bay

Opened 1866 Closed 1966
SHANKLIN

Luccombe

Opened 1900 Closed 1952
VENTNOR TOWN
Bonchurch
St. Bonif. Down
VENTNOR
Tunnel
ST. LAWRENCE
Tunnel
Niton

WROXALL

Apuldurcombe

WHITWELL

Chale

St. Catharines Pt.

Opened 1862 Closed 1966
Opened 1875 Closed 1966
HAVEN STREET
WHIPPINGHAM
WOOTTON
Tunnel
PAN LANE

Opened 1879 Closed 1956
ASHEY
Nunwell

NEWCHURCH
Arreton
HORRINGFORD
ALVERSTONE
Opened 1875 Closed 1956
Lake

Apse Manor

Opened 1897 Closed 1952
GODSHILL

MERSTONE

SHIDE

BLACKWATER

Opened 1880 Closed 1959

NEWPORT
CARISBROOKE
WATCHINGWELL (PRIVATE)

CEMENT MILLS HALT
Parkhurst
MILLHILL
COWES
MEDINA WHARF
R. Osborne
R. Medina

THE SOLENT

Beaulieu River

Newtown Bay

Shalfleet

CALBOURNE & SHALFLEET
NINGWOOD
Swainston
Calbourne

The Back of the Wight
Shorwell
Brighstone

Brook

Opened 1889 Closed 1953
FRESHWATER
Freshwater Bay

Proposed Tunnel

YARMOUTH

Keyhaven

Colwell Bay
Totland Bay
Alum Bay
The Needles

BROCKENHURST

LYMINGTON (TOWN)
LYMINGTON (PIER)

ENGLISH CHANNEL

Scale in Miles
0 1 2 3 4

Formerly Isle of Wight Railway
    "   Isle of Wight Central Railway
    "   Freshwater, Yarmouth & Newport Rly.
    "   L.&S.W.R. & L.B.&S.C. Joint Lines
    "   L.&S.W.R.

N

Introduction

The aim of the authors is to give a broad picture, amply illustrated, of how the railways of the Isle of Wight looked—and were—during the 105 years of steam operation which ended on December 31, 1966. The service now remaining, London tube stock shuttling between Ryde Pier and Shanklin, can be left to other pens.

This book does not set out to be a detailed history of the Island lines nor to give a detailed technical description of the rolling stock. This has been done in Michael Robbins's excellent book published in 1953 and brought up to date in 1966. Moreover, it was once attempted nearly 40 years ago by one of the authors while the other was frustrated by Hitler from such a work. There is not much either of Parliamentary or of financial matters nor a history of the various steamship companies who started to run ferries to the Island from the early 1800s. There are, however, references to the steamers in the text.

The Isle of Wight has always been a place apart—from being an island of course—and its countryside and villages and farms still manage, with some difficulty perhaps, to retain a degree of charm which has always distinguished the Island from the mainland. The little towns, especially when inundated by the holiday crowds, are less attractive with their fun fairs, bingo parlours, casinos and caravan camps, but this season is short—all too short for prosperity indeed—and for nine months of the year even they have a pleasant Victorian air.

The countryside, the downs and the south-west coast are splendid Channel-coast scenery, as good as any in the south of England with one or two spots which qualify as superb.

The Island is just big enough to take some knowing, 23 by 13 miles with a coastline of 60 miles shaped like a diamond, and just small enough to be learned and loved in due time. Like golf, if it were easier it wouldn't be worth playing and if it were harder you couldn't play it. Into this setting the railways have fitted with individuality and charm.

Starting with a little 4¼-mile line from Cowes to Newport in 1862 the system grew to a maximum of 55½ miles by 1900 with one or two rather lame-duck branches and the whole never a prosperous affair. When amalgamation came along in 1923 there were five separate railway undertakings in the Island. The Isle of Wight Railway ran along the eastern seaboard; the Isle of Wight Central radiated from Newport, the Island capital in the centre, to Ryde, Cowes, Sandown and Ventnor, and the Freshwater, Yarmouth & Newport ran from Newport out to the western end of the Island. Then there were the joint lines, without rolling stock, of the London & South Western and London, Brighton & South Coast Railways between Ryde St John's Road and Ryde Pier Head and finally there was the London & South Western station, though no railway, at Yarmouth pier. All this was no more than a Victorian survival but of course paradise for the railway enthusiast even if less amusing for the traveller.

The amalgamation of this whole mixture into the Southern Railway gave at last the chance to sort things out and the Island railways greatly improved, passing rapidly through, as it were, an Edwardian period in the late 1920s and by the 1930s reaching standards of punctuality, frequency of service, speed and cleanliness fully up to date and unequalled anywhere in Britain; spotless rolling stock, lovingly tended, a service of unequalled density for single line

5

working, pride in the job and a relish for it were the characteristics of those days. After the war these things continued for a little but then it was suddenly evening. From being a smart little railway operation it became quaint, then run down and finally a total anachronism, attractive only to railway enthusiasts. Perhaps the economic facts of life ran against railways and little steam railways especially, perhaps the heart went out of things, perhaps this and perhaps that but very soon after British Railways were formed the writing was on the wall. In Southern times the whole system was kept in being, under nationalized management things were or perhaps just looked different. Truncation came, with threats of utter closure and the last final days of decline with grubby coaches and dirty neglected little engines were a pitiful contrast with the brave days of even 1947 when malachite green, burnished brass and even lined-out wheels proclaimed a belief in the future, in doing things well and being proud of it.

Yet for all the standardization, the black paint and inferior heraldic emblems, the upper-quadrant signals and the lack of first-class compartments, the Island railways somehow maintained some shreds of individual character to the end, the panting Westinghouse brake-pumps, the hoarse hooters and until nearly the end attention to cleanliness and the polished nameplates of the engines made them something different and apart.

What we have tried to do is to give some personal reminiscence and sense of atmosphere together with as good a collection of pictures as could be found, many of which, we are glad to say, have never been published before. If any of our love for the Island and its little railways has come through the words and communicated itself to our readers we will feel happy indeed.

CHAPTER 1

Early Days

The family used to go down to the Isle of Wight for holidays either by the Brighton line from Leatherhead—usually behind a front-coupled *Gladstone*—or, if we were heading for the western end of the Island, by the South Western. This, compared with the direct run to Portsmouth, was a fairly complicated journey but none the less an enjoyable one for children.

We used to start out on the South Western, amid the early businessmen, travelling in a brownish-upholstered, second-class carriage; we used to think the stock on this line was much ahead of that on the rival LBSCR in which in winter the carriages would have flat cans of hot water in them to rest and warm your feet on. We would leave Leatherhead behind an M7 0–4–4 tank or else a Jubilee 0–4–2 tender engine, getting out at Wimbledon to cross to another platform and to wait for the down semi-fast to take us to Hampshire. Nearly always this train was led by a double-single, of one Mr Drummond's strange 4–2–2–os—No. 369 or 373 as often as not—with a rake of salmon-pink and brown bogie coaches. This train moved sedately with stops at Surbiton, Woking, Farnborough, Basingstoke, Winchester to Eastleigh where memory seems to introduce another change, then Southampton and running on through the first fringes of the New Forest to Brockenhurst where we got out. Between Southampton and Redbridge there was always the hope that a red 4–4–0 of the Midland and South Western Junction Railway might be seen.

This journey in 1914, a day or so after the war began, is a vivid memory still with soldiers guarding the bridges and my father throwing newspapers out of the train window for them. A night or so later we witnessed the capture, in the narrows of the Solent, of a German ship, which, unconscious of the outbreak of war, had entered forbidden waters and had been fired on from one of the forts on the cliffs above Totland Bay.

At Brockenhurst we would get into the local train and rattle off behind an M7 down the single line branch to Lymington, stopping for a moment at the Town station and then out to the Pier. This was always a great moment of the holiday as from here you could see the hills of western Wight across the sky beyond the flats and marshes of the Lymington River with the Tennyson monument on the highest point of the downs. So aboard the *Solent* with her buff funnel, the flagship of the fleet, and off we'd go past the older *Lymington* at the Pier, down the curling muddy river and then out into the Solent with Hurst Castle striking out from the Hampshire shore and the Needles at the end of the Island briefly in view. Of course, an essential part of the entertainment was a visit to the engine room with its warm oily smell where the majestic surge and heave of the great rods and the slow breathing sounds of the cylinders was a quiet contrast to the fussy thud-thud-thud of the paddle wheels outside.

By now Yarmouth would be approaching with its square-towered church and castle at the water's edge and, in 1916, 1917 and 1918, the old gunboat *Magpie* and a flotilla of ancient torpedo-boats for submarine patrol moored just off-shore. We would tie up at the pier head and our luggage was trundled down on a hand-truck while we walked down the planks to the little town.

Sometimes, just before we reached Yarmouth pier, a little trail of steam would betray a Freshwater train crossing the marshes of the Western Yar, our first sight of an Island railway.

We got a great liking for the old paddle-boats of the South Western and frequently took an afternoon round trip from Yarmouth; down to Totland Bay first, then across to Lymington, wondering about those strange towers at Sway near the mainland shore; at Lymington we would wait for the London train to come in and then steam back to Yarmouth in time for supper. Sitting on the deck at the far stern between the rudder chains on a fair summer afternoon was an approximation to bliss. Tea was part of the outing with a special type of flat round bun, rather yellow, with coarse sugar crystals on top.

The Portsmouth route had its pleasures too, especially the dockyard and the grey naval vessels coming in and out—the destroyers giving the wildest whoop-whoop-whoop on their sirens—and moving about inside the harbour naval pinnaces with burnished brass funnels and the little Gosport ferries, some of them still running today fifty years later, a group of which then had purple funnels, which came and went beneath the very skirts of the Isle of Wight 'Duchesses'.

The Great Naval Review of 1914 is an indelible memory; mile upon mile of vast ships as far as you could see to either horizon, through which we steamed in an excursion paddle steamer, the white-funnelled *Balmoral* perhaps, from Southampton to Portsmouth.

The boats to Ryde were bigger and more sophisticated than the Lymington paddlers; you had to pay 6d to a man in a peaked cap to get a blue ticket to use the upper-deck, for example, but the surge and sigh of the engine room was the same[1] and there was certainly a lot to see, warships on the move and the odd forts out in Spithead had to be noted down and then Ryde began to loom up with the great spire of All Saints' Church dominating the town from its hill. The dark mass of the half-mile pier with its huddle of buildings became clearer; a plume of steam showed that one of the boat trains was already in and then another flash of steam at the root of the pier darting out of the tunnel by the esplanade betrayed the arrival of the other. We would queue with high impatience to get off the boat down the narrow gangways while the luggage in trucks was slung ashore by the steam-cranes on the pier, for by this time we could see the Isle of Wight Railway train simmering at Platform One, a trim symmetrical rake of brown coaches and a red engine at the head, which one of course we needed to know. All you

---

[1] Anyone who wishes to experience this bygone atmosphere can find it on the occasional trips made by the last surviving paddle steamer in Great Britain, the *Waverley*.

1. A very early view of *Ryde* with its nameplate on the boiler. This engine hauled the first train on the Isle of Wight Railway, August 23, 1864

2. An early photograph at Ventnor, probably in the eighties. The locomotive still has the original boiler with the dome over the firebox, though the cab has been added

3. Coming up from Sandown about 1900; Newport train approaching Merstone with IWCR single-wheeler tank engine

4. Old No. 2 of the Isle of Wight Central in the 1890s; she and her sister *Pioneer* were the first engines in the Island

5. IWCR 0–4–2 tank engine No. 3 formerly of the Cowes and Newport Railway. She worked for years at Medina Wharf but ended her days in the Island struggling to provide a motor train service with the huge Midland coach

6. IWCR No. 3 ex Cowes & Newport Railway, built by Black Hawthorn for the contractor in 1870. It is standing in Newport station about 1905 with two former Isle of Wight (Newport Junction) carriages of 1875

7. The opening train for the Newport, Godshill and St Lawrence line on July 19, 1897. Mr C. L. Conach in top-hat looks every inch a General Manager. The locomotive is No. 6

8. An early picture at Bembridge, possibly on opening day, May 27, 1882. The engine is the *Bembria* which ran the branch for many years

could see was that it wasn't big *Bonchurch* or *Brading* because you could just see a round window in the back of the cab but whether it was *Ryde, Ventnor, Sandown, Shanklin* or *Wroxall* was too difficult at that range.

Meanwhile, a hoarse hooter told us that the Isle of Wight Central train at least wasn't hauled by an ex-Brighton 'Terrier' but you couldn't see until you'd left the boat and got inside the station that 2–4–0 tank No. 7 was in charge and heading a pretty mixed collection of coaches.

We would then board the Ventnor train, taking seats in an eight-wheeled non-bogie coach which had once trundled round the Metropolitan tunnels of London; then with a fearful high-pitched shriek from *Shanklin* we'd be off rumbling down the pier tracks to the shore. As often as not the Central train for Newport and Cowes, the engine running bunker first while ours ran chimney first, would catch us up at Ryde St John's Road station. From here two tracks ran side by side for nearly a mile to Smallbrook before swinging apart and the trains would sometimes run together with suitable exchanges emanating from the rolling stock until they parted. Although these tracks made no contact south of St John's Road and one was used exclusively by the Isle of Wight Central Railway, they were in fact both owned by the Isle of Wight Railway.

Our Isle of Wight Railway train was now in thick woodland, emerging at Brading where the two-coach branch train for Bembridge behind another 2–4–0 tank—for the little Manning Wardle 0–6–0 had gone to the wars and never came back—was waiting to meet the Boat Train. So along the flat lands of the Eastern Yar to Sandown where the Isle of Wight Railway had its head office. Here we could just get a sight of an Isle of Wight Central train at the far platform, in charge of 2–4–0T No. 8 with its covered bunker and huge cab, before the view was blotted out by the big bunker of *Bonchurch* heading north for Ryde with another IWR train of Metropolitan stock behind her.

After Sandown some big climbing began, past Lake, past Merry Gardens where the Three Little Pigs had got into such trouble with the Big Bad Wolf when they went to the fair at Shanklin, with a glimpse across to the west to that delightful ridge of Downs with the thin pillar of the monument erected to commemorate the visit of Alexander I, Emperor of All the Russias to the Island in 1814, showing high on St Catherine's Down above Whitwell. So to Shanklin station itself, then storming on up Apse Bank, the great smooth curve of St Boniface Down loomed up ahead and soon after Wroxall we were under it in a dark mephitic tunnel three-quarters of a mile long from which we emerged right in Ventnor station, carved out of the chalk of the Down itself. In building this tunnel a spring was tapped which provided the water supply for Ventnor—and does to this day. Crossing from our island platform on a moveable gangway to the main station there was just time to see *Shanklin* move on to the turn-table points at the end of the line to take water and prepare to run round the train for the return trip before parental impatience commanded us to the horse-cab and our hotel.

Meanwhile, the Central train we had parted from at Ryde had been working its way across to Newport with stops at Ashey, which most improbably had a primitive racecourse where no meeting ever seemed imminent, Haven Street, Wootton and finally Whippingham with a better-than-average station as it used to serve Osborne House; in fact the stations at Ashey and Whippingham were mirror-images of each other. Along this line from Ashey, the railway ran mostly in thick woodland until after Whippingham it came quite close to East Cowes, then swinging south ran down the east side of the Medina River, hooter braying, into the shortest tunnel on record and over a moveable span bridge, over the Medina, where it joined the

IWCR branch from Sandown and into what always seemed the great network of tracks and lines at Newport. Here there usually seemed to be too much to see, especially if one had to catch the Freshwater, Yarmouth & Newport train standing in its bay with an immaculate bright-green-and-polished-copper 'Terrier' facing you. Usually you could see the fantastic old twelve-wheeled Midland coach with a clerestory parked in a siding. A train would come in from Cowes for Sandown, possibly with that most handsome engine, the outside cylindered 4–4–0 tank No. 6 on it or a little train of four-wheelers for Ventnor Town via Merstone and the Undercliff led by 'Terrier' No. 11 which once, so long ago, had won a gold medal at an exhibition in Paris. The Central trains in those days had a red destination board with white letters at the locomotive chimney-base while the IWR engines carried a white disc with a green centre when on the main line or a lamp if on the Bembridge branch. The Invalids' Special which the IWR ran for a time non-stop from Ryde to Ventnor in the nineties appropriately carried a red disc with a white cross.

Backing out of Newport in the Freshwater train there were always a couple of IWC engines to be seen around the shed and shops, perhaps one of that anaemic pair No. 4 or No. 5 built in 1876 for the Ryde & Newport Railway and almost certainly another of the four 'Terriers' with a goods train coming in from Medina Wharf. Then, pulling forward on to the FYN line and past the separate station, which had necessitated a walk from the IWCR for some years during an unhappy period of friction, you were off for the west, out over the rumbling Town Gate viaduct and on to Carisbrooke, with a fine view of the castle on the hill. On the train would go through woods and fields with the spine of central hills always overlooking it on the left, the six-wheeled tank engine making a characteristic der-der-dér, der-der-dér, der-der-dér noise over the rail joints or clattering over Calbourne viaduct while the four-wheelers, hastily sent from Manchester when the FYN and IWCR broke off their friendship in 1913, rumbled and nattered behind. Past Watchingwell, the private station where one rarely stopped, up and down an almost switchback route to Calbourne and Ningwood and then here again was dear friendly Yarmouth, showing from the railway the least attractive view of that nice engaging town.

In the period of which we have been writing, 1915–22, the locomotive stock in the Island was extraordinarily interesting. The Isle of Wight Railway still had its complete stud of Beyer Peacock 2–4–0 tanks and its only loss since it had opened in 1864 was the little *Bembridge* which had gone to Mesopotamia on war duties. The seven 2–4–0 tanks, although four of them were over fifty years old at the end of the war, were an attractive group, no two exactly alike though the differences were often very subtle, confused for the unobservant by an exchange of boilers by *Ryde* and *Shanklin* just after World War I.

The first three, *Ryde*, *Sandown* and *Shanklin* when delivered in 1864 had dome and safety valves over the firebox, an open footplate without cab and a vast medieval copper-capped chimney. So did *Ventnor* added in 1868; but the later additions, *Wroxall* in 1872 and *Brading* in 1876 had cabs from the start and dome and spring balance safety valves in the centre of the boiler. *Brading* was a slightly bigger engine and for some reason had two rectangular rear windows where the other five had three round ones. *Bonchurch* of 1883 was an altogether bigger and heavier engine, with Ramsbottom safety valves on the firebox top, a plain dome and an outside coal bunker. She was notorious for having fallen off the lighter which was delivering her at Brading Harbour and so spent some days under the sea.

In their heyday before World War I these engines were resplendent with polished copper and brass setting off their dark red paint in a most handsome way; they then had shorter

and 10. Isle of Wight Central power. The upper picture shows 4–4–0 tank No. 6 when new in 1890.
ne lower shows 4–4–0 tank No. 7 at Freshwater; she came from the North London Railway in 1880

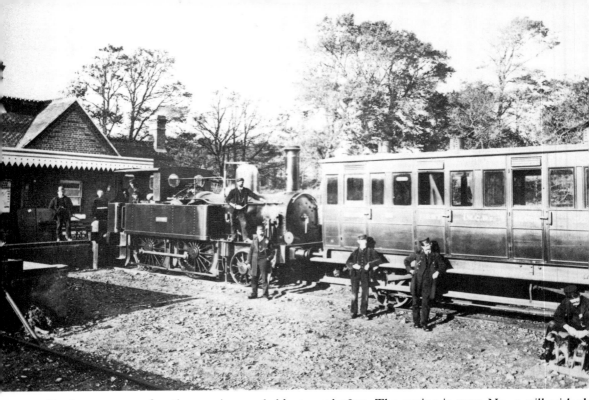

11. Freshwater soon after the opening, probably around 1890. The engine is IWCR No. 5 still with th
name *Osborne* and a couple of dogs have come along too

12. No. 5 again but with the nameplates gone. She is here in the cutting near St Lawrence in about 19c

In 1906 rail-motors were in fashion so the IWCR acquired one. It was not a success and the parts were arated; the coach survived thirty years but the engine was sold in 1917

Another rail-motor attempt. No. 3, IWCR, encumbered with sheet-steel cladding pushes the old dland twelve-wheel coach along the Undercliff

15. A rare bird. Photographs of the second IWCR No. 2 are few and far between. This heavy engine, ev
with cut-down tanks, was unsatisfactory. Pictured near Ventnor Town in 1910

16. Alverstone station, on the Sandown line, with the famous 'Terrier' No. 11 heading the train

17. Building the railway pier at Ryde probably in 1879

8. *Shanklin* taking Ventnor train down the 1 in 50 from Ryde Esplanade in 1913. The engine still has
~~~er copper-capped chimney but the dome is painted over and the tank hand-rails are gone

19. One of Dr Tice Budden's best. The train is leaving Wroxall in 1900 and the locomotive is *Sandow* or *Shanklin*

20. The exit of Ventnor tunnel has been a photographic favourite for years. Here is *Shanklin* emerging in pre-war 'full-dress' in 1910

chimneys than the original but with copper tops, and brass bell-mouthed domes and polished handrails above the tanks. By the end of the war much of the glory had departed with the handrails and bell mouths gone, the domes painted over, save that *Bonchurch* still had a battered brass dome, but by some piece of skill a highly attractive cast-iron chimney was devised at Ryde shops which set off these sturdy little ponies admirably. Later, starting in 1920, a less attractive cut down chimney was introduced by Mr Tahourdin with a bigger rim. Such was the quality of these little engines that the Southern took them all on in 1923 except for *Sandown* which was scrapped with a cracked frame; the last of them, *Wroxall* survived until 1933. *Ryde*, the first of them, was withdrawn in 1932 and some hopes were held that she might be preserved but in those hard times no one would come up to scratch and she was eventually cut up.

The Isle of Wight Central engines of this period were a much more mixed lot. Towards the end of World War I, the original singles of the Cowes & Newport had long been gone and so had the ex-North London inside-cylinder 4–4–0 tank; long since scrapped too was the strange single driver well-tank off the Furness which had been the sole engine of the Isle of Wight (Newport Junction) Railway apart from a Beattie 2–2–2T hired from the London & South Western. But we can remember seeing late in the war at the back of the goods yard at Newport the second No. 1, the minuscule 0–4–0 bought to run the unsuccessful railcar of which the coach portion long survived, and Cowes & Newport No. 3 the 0–4–2 saddle tank which did some motor-train duties with the Midland twelve-wheeled coach in tow, both waiting for shipment to Tees-side for their last dying efforts as industrial shunters. The railcar had been bought in 1906 when they were highly fashionable but it was given up by the IWCR in 1911 as passengers complained of excessive oscillation in the coach. Late in World War I the big 0–4–4 tank, the second No. 2 was still running, although soon destined to go back to the northeast from which she had come. Otherwise, at the end of the war, they were all there; the little 1876 Beyer Peacock 2–4–0 tanks Nos 4 and 5 from the Ryde & Newport, smaller and flimsier than their IWR cousins, the slightly bigger No. 8 with its great enveloping cab and the still bigger broader-hipped No. 7 from the Midland & South Western Junction—which was given a new boiler with Ramsbottom safety valves in 1920. But the pride of the fleet was undoubtedly the big 4–4–0 outside-cylinder Black Hawthorn tank which looked so very much better with its thin locally-cast chimney than with its coarse original. Lastly, the Central had four 'Terriers' 9, 10, 11 and 12 with enlarged bunkers and these had wonderful careers, some totalling ninety years of life and ending their days on the mainland when the Isle of Wight needed them no more. It is good to be able to report that although Nos 9, 10 and 12 eventually went for scrap the famous No. 11, the most renowned of all the Stroudley 'Terriers' somehow has survived and after Hayling Island service as BR No. 32640 and temporary retirement at Butlin's, Pwllheli, is again on the Isle of Wight. This little engine, in the full glory of Stroudley's elaborately lined-out yellow paint, caused something of a sensation at the Paris Exhibition in 1878 where she got a gold medal; on the subsequent trial run on the Western of France line to Dieppe, with her negro fireman stoking, she surprised her French hosts with her speed and acceleration. Except for IWCR Nos 4 and 6 all these engines wore the Southern green and even No. 6 which alas was early condemned, carried a green SR number plate on her bunker before she died. On the IWC at the end of World War I as on the IWR, brass and copper trim were out, the last surviving copper-topped chimney being on No. 4 in 1919, but the IWC, like its rival, contrived to produce a most elegant plain chimney cast by Wheeler & Hurst in Newport, which suited these little creatures very well. The IWC livery which had been red until 1910 was at this time black lined-out with red and white.

21

The Freshwater line which had to conjure up some motive power in a hurry in 1913—with a Solent tunnel a possibility, Sir Sam Fay and the Great Central were taking an interest here—laid hands on two 0–6–0 tanks and some four-wheeled coaches from the Manchester, South Junction & Altrincham Railway.[1] No. 1 of the FYN was a tough little Manning Wardle engine used on constructing the GW & GC joint line from Northolt to High Wycombe and had the distinction, except for the short service 0–4–0 railcar locomotive on the IWC, of being the latest built of all the engines to run in the Island during the 105 years of steam operation and the only one built in the twentieth century.[2] No. 1 lasted for quite a few years of the Southern régime.

FYN No. 2 had an even more romantic career. She was born No. 46 *Newington* in 1876, one of two 'Terriers' bought from the Brighton line by the London & South Western Railway for the Lyme Regis branch in 1903; she arrived in the Island in 1913 with a Drummond boiler with safety valves in the dome, the original copper-topped chimney and still wearing 'LSWR' on her tank sides, with the number 734. She was fitted with the vacuum brake in her FYN days, a relic of her LSWR ownership; in consequence she could only work with one set of FYN coaches. No. 1, on the other hand, had both the vacuum and the Westinghouse brakes so that she was equally at home with either of the sets of FYN passenger stock. No. 2 remained in alien livery until 1919 when she emerged resplendent from an overhaul in brilliant grass-green paint lined-out in black and white and lettered 'FYN', with scarlet side rods; she looked superb. She was taken into the Southern stock in 1923 as W2, was later given the name *Freshwater*, and was then renumbered in the Island W8. She went back to the mainland to the Hayling Island branch in 1949 as No. 32646 (she would have been No. 646 in the Brighton books if she had remained with them up to the amalgamation and 2646 afterwards in the Southern register) and worked there until the branch closed in November 1963. The Sadler Rail Coach Company bought her and moved her to Droxford on the old Meon Valley line where she worked until Brickwoods, the Portsmouth brewers, bought her. In the year of Our Lord 1966, over ninety years old, she steamed her last and reposed in honoured retirement on Hayling Island, restored to Brighton yellow and copper trim, on a plinth outside a Public House called the 'Hayling Billy'. But retirement was not to last, for in 1979 No. 46 or FYN No. 2 or W8, whatever you call her, returned to the Island for restoration as W8. She and the famous *Brighton* are the last survivors of all the Island companies' engines.

The Freshwater line also had a 20 h.p. Drewry twelve-seater petrol-driven railcar which by 1919 ran the only non-stop service in the Island, 'limited' to 'mainland passengers only' passing all stations between Yarmouth and Newport.

It is of some interest to speculate what might have happened if the amalgamation of 1923 hadn't occurred or if the Island lines themselves had coalesced or if as was at one time suggested, they had been taken over by the LBSC and LSW jointly, like the line between Ryde Pier Head and St John's Road and the Portsmouth–Ryde boats.

Certainly the Island lines were short of power, and of coaches, before 1923 and there was a rumour that the IWR was going to hire some small 0–4–4 tanks of the O2 class from the

[1] Was it, we wonder, of the former occupants of these coaches that this immortal verse was written:
'They sleep in Hale and Sale by night, in Manchester by day;
They travel by the C.L.C. and M.S.J. & A.'

[2] The E4 0–6–2 tank No. 2510 (formerly *Twineham*) which made a brief appearance after World War II just fits into this description for she was built in December 1900.

21. *Ryde* at Ventnor in 1900 when she had a second dome over the firebox

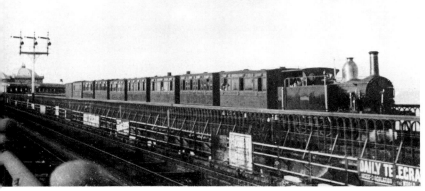

22. *Sandown* on Ryde Pier probably about 1900

23. The 'Invalids' Express', with its special head code, speeding through Shanklin behind *Wroxall*, picture about 1895

24 and 25. Two sisters at Newport; Nos 4 and 5 in 1919. These engines belonged to the Ryde and Newport Railway and No. 4 carries the last copper-capped chimney on the IWCR albeit painted over

26. IWCR No. 3 later sold to the North East Coast in 1918 as an industrial shunter

27. The Pride of the Fleet: Isle of Wight Central 4–4–0 T No. 6 in 1922 much improved by her locally-cast chimney

28 and 29. Two more Beyer Peacock 2–4–0 tank engines on the Isle of Wight Central in 1920–1. No. 7 w
bought from the Midland & South Western Junction and No. 8 was obtained new.

30. *Upper* Manning Wardle 0–6–0 tank No. 1

31. *Centre* 20 h.p. Drewry petrol railcar

32. *Lower* Ex LSWR 'Terrier' No. 2. The photographs date from 1919–20

33. *Ventnor* of the Isle of Wight Railway on the turntable points at Ventnor in August 1919

34. *Shanklin* waits in the summer sun at Ryde Pier Head for the boat to arrive; August 1919

RYDE NEWPORT AND COWES AND ISLE OF WIGHT (NEWPORT JUNCTION) RAILWAYS

ISLE OF WIGHT RACES

Tuesday, April 22nd, Flat and Hurdle Racing
WEDNESDAY, APRIL 23rd, STEEPLE CHASES,

AT ASHEY

AND IMMEDIATELY ADJOINING THE STATION,
(FIRST RACE AT 1-30 EACH DAY.)

Boat & Train Services on both days will run as under from Southampton, Cowes, Newport, Ryde, Portsmouth, Ventnor, Shanklin, Sandown, &c

Special trains from Ryde to Ashey and vice versa, in connection with the trains to and from Sandown, Shanklin, Ventnor, &c

Portsmouth, Ryde, and Ashey.

Portsmouth Harbour	dep	9 45		10 55		12 10	1 20
Victoria Pier	dep	9 20		11 0		12 15	
Southsea Pier	dep	9 30		11 10		12 20	1 30
Ryde (Pier Head)	dep	10 43		11 50	12 25	1 0	1 50
Ryde (Esplanade)	dep	10 45		11 54	12 29	1 4	1 54
Ryde (St. John's road)	dep	10 50	11 5	12 0	12 34	1 8	1 56
Ashey	arr	10 55	11 12	12 7	12 41	1 15	2 4

Ashey	dep	5 20	5 54	6 30	7 57
Ryde (St. John's road)	dep	5 25	6 2	6 35	8 5
Ryde (Esplanade)	dep	5 30	6 6	6 39	8 9
Ryde (Pier Head)	dep	5 35	6 9	6 43	8 13
Portsmouth	arr	6 30	6 30		9 40

CHEAP TICKETS FROM PORTSMOUTH PIERS.　　**RETURN FARES—1st CLASS, 3s.6d.　　2nd CLASS, 2s.6d.**

VENTNOR, SHANKLIN, SANDOWN, & ASHEY.

Ventnor	dep	10 23	12 6	1 12
Wroxall	dep	10 29	12 6	1 18
Shanklin	dep	10 36	12 13	1 25
Sandown	dep	10 43	12 26	1 32
Ryde (St. John's road)	arr	10 57	12 34	1 46
Ashey	arr	11 12	12 40	2 4

Ashey	dep	5 20	5 54	6 30
Ryde (St. John's road)	dep	5 39	6 45	6 45
Sandown	arr	5 53	6 59	6 59
Shanklin	arr	5 59	7 5	7 5
Wroxall	arr	6 6	7 12	7 12
Ventnor	arr	6 12	7 19	7 19

THROUGH CARRIAGES from VENTNOR, WROXALL, SHANKLIN, & SANDOWN to ASHEY--Fares as under

SOUTHAMPTON, COWES, NEWPORT, AND ASHEY.

Southampton	dep	8 30			11 15		
Cowes	dep	9 55		11 47	12 20	12 35	
Newport	dep	10 15	10 35	12 0	12 30	1 15	
Ashey	arr	10 35	10 56	12 25	12 45	1 41	

Ashey	dep	5 25	5 54	6 30	7 57
Newport	arr	5 30	6 14	6 50	8 19
Cowes	arr	5 50	6 41	7 10	8 56
Southampton	arr	7 0			

All Trains between Cowes, Newport, and Ashey will call at intermediate Stations, the 12-30, p.m., Newport to Ashey and 5-25, p.m., Ashey to Cowes, (which will call at Newport and Cowes only) excepted

Through Return Railway Fares Southampton, Portsmouth, Cowes, Ventnor, Wroxall, Shanklin, Sandown, and Ryde to Ashey as under—

	1st class s. d.	2nd class s. d.		1st class s. d.	2nd class s. d.		1st class s. d.	2nd class s. d.
From Southampton	4 4	3 1	From Shanklin	2 9	1 9	From Ryde (St. John's rd)	-- 10	-- 8
„ Cowes	2 6	2 0	„ Sandown	2 0	1 6	„ Ryde (Esplanade)	1 4	1 1
„ Ventnor	3 9	3 0	„ Brading	1 9	1 3	„ Ryde (Pier Head)	1 10	1 6
„ Wroxall	3 3	2 9	„ Portsmouth	3 6	2 8	„ Newport	2 3	1 6

Newport, I.W., March, 1884.　　　　　　　　　　　　　　　　　　　　H. SIMMONS, Manager.

T. KENTFIELD, MACHINE PRINTER, PYLE STREET, NEWPORT.

COMBINED
RAIL & COACH EXCURSION
TO
BLACKGANG,

Through the beautiful and unrivalled scenery of the
RENOWNED UNDERCLIFF.

EVERY WEEK-DAY

A well appointed Coach or other conveyance will leave

VENTNOR STATION

on arrival of the Train due at 11.8 a.m. and convey Passengers through the

BEAUTIFUL UNDERCLIFF

To BLACKGANG

(For the famous Chine),

allowing time for luncheon and returning at 2.45 p.m., connecting with the 4.40 p.m. and 5.33 p.m. Trains from Ventnor Station (on return journey Passengers will be put down in the Town).

Bookings as under :—

FROM			TRAIN	RETURN FARES (including Rail and Coach).	
			a.m.	1st Class.	2nd Class.
Ryde (Pier Head)	...	dep.	10 26	5 -	3/10
Ryde (Esplanade)	...	,,	10 30	4 10	3/9
,, (St. John's Road)	...	,,	10 34		
Bembridge	...	,,	10 30		
St. Helen's	...	,,	10 35	4/-	3/-
Brading	...	,,	10 42		
Sandown	...	,,	10 48		
Shanklin	...	,,	10 54	3 6	2 6
Wroxall	...	,,	11 2	2 3	2 0
Ventnor (by Coach)	...	,,	11 20		
Blackgang (by Coach)	...	arr.	12 50		

CHILDREN HALF PRICE.

N.B.—The road conveyance is not under the control of the Company, and the tickets granted for the Coach portion of the route are issued by the Isle of Wight Railway Company solely as Agents for and on behalf of the proprietors of the Coach and on the express condition that the Company is not to be responsible for any injury, damage, loss or detention whatsoever to Passengers or to luggage during or in respect of the transit by the road conveyance.

Joint Railway Companies' Steam Packet Service

COLLIERS' STRIKE

The Joint Railway Companies give PUBLIC NOTICE that in consequence of the Strike

The Service of Steam Packets
between
Portsmouth Harbour,
Southsea Pier and Ryde

advertised to run from 1st October 1911 to 31st May 1912, will be cancelled on

Wednesday 13th March, 1912.

The undermentioned service will be run on and from that date, until further notice, (weather and other circumstances permitting) :—

Portsmouth and Southsea to Ryde							Week Days		
	Mail								
Ports. Hbr. dep.	2.40	8.15	9.45	12.15	1.15	1.55	3.25	6. 5	8.1
Southsea Pier	...	...	9.55	12.25	1.25		3.35	6.15	8.2
Ryde Pier arr.	3.10	8.45	10.20	12.50	1.50	2.25	4.0	6.40	8.4

Ryde to Southsea and Portsmouth						Week Days		
Ryde Pier dep.	8.0	10.10	12.55	1.55	4.5	6.18	6.45	9.2
Southsea Pier arr.	8.25	10.35	1.20	...	...	7.10	...	
Ports. Hbr. ,,	8.35	10.45	1.30	2.25	4.35	6.48	...	9.5

Portsmouth & Southsea to Ryde. (Sundays)					Ryde to Southsea & Portsmou			
Ports. H. dep.	2.40	10.10	12.10	2.10	6.45	Ryde P. dep.	11.0	1.0	5.0	9.4
S'sea P.	...	10.20	12.20	2.20	6.55	S'sea P. arr.	11.25	1.25	5.25	...
Ryde P. arr.	3.10	10.45	12.45	2.45	7.20	Ports. H. ,,	11.35	1.35	5.35	9.5

(A) Southampton and Isle of Wight Steam Packet Co.'s Steamer. Passengers holding Railway Companies Tickets may travel from Portsmouth Harbour and Southsea Pier to Ryde by this Steamer.

THE TOW BOAT SERVICE between Portsmouth and Ryde will be run on Mondays, Wednesdays and Fridays only.

Excursion of 1907

Trouble in 1912

In the year of the Triangular Tournament

I.W. Central Rly

CRICKET MATCH AT PORTSMOUTH

AUSTRALIAN.
V.
HAMPSHIRE
22nd, 23rd and 24th JULY, 1912.

CHEAP EXCURSION TICKET
TO
PORTSMOUTH Hbr. or SOUTHSEA PIER
(Via RYDE)

By any Train due to leave before 3-30 p.m.

FROM	1st. Return.	3rd Return
Any I.W. Central Station (except the undermentioned)	3/6	2/6
Freshwater, Yarmouth, Ningwood, and Calbourne	4/6	3/6
Carisbrooke - - -	4/-	3/-

LSWR with an eye to purchase. This rumour was probably generated by the negotiations which had been going on ever since the Railway Act of 1921 for the LSWR to take over the IWR. The first offer of the LSWR in 1921 was turned down by the IWR board on May 20, 1922. An amended offer was made which the IWR directors were willing to recommend their stockholders to accept, in a letter dated June 21, 1922; this if agreed would have meant a take-over of the Isle of Wight Railway by the LSWR on January 1, 1923. However, in the event the amalgamation took place and supplanted this lesser deal. Certainly two of these O2 tanks, the first of no less than twenty-three, appeared with surprising suddenness in May 1923.

Probably locomotive and coach development would not have gone very differently from the way it did as limitations of dimensions and weight imposed severe restrictions as was shown when the big 0-6-2 tank of class E4 was briefly introduced in 1947-8; so no doubt the O2s and the E1 0-6-0s and the 'Terriers' would have been used anyway, though it is nice to picture a few of those charming Brighton 0-4-4 tanks with their tall Billinton chimneys in IWR red as *St Helens, Niton* or *Blackgang*[1] or perhaps, loading gauge permitting, a South Eastern H-class 0-4-4 tank with its curly cab and bunker on the Central.

We wish it were possible to be as informed on the coaching stock of the Island railways as on the locomotives but the lack of knowledge is severe. The IWR had its eighteen Metropolitan eight-wheeled coaches, the bodies of eleven of which later reposed on the sea wall at St Helen's, and some six-wheelers it used on the Bembridge branch which once had been four-wheelers on the Ryde Pier tramway and were finally converted into six-wheeled brake vans; the IWR also had some four-wheeled coaches which came from the North London with splendid first-class compartments with two back-to-back arm-chairs in each. The Central had a couple of small bogie coaches built for it new in 1889 and of course the 1875 Midland twelve-wheeler bought in 1907 to make a motor-train. The FYN had its MSJ & A stock but whence and when all the rest of the ramshackle collection of four-wheelers came to the Island is a confused mystery. Some coaches on the Central certainly came second-hand from the Great Eastern and some from the London & North Western built in 1854. Other Central coaches came from the South Western and from the Brighton.

The geography of the railways had of course been fixed well before the Kaiser's war broke out: the Cowes & Newport began construction in 1859 and opened in 1862; the IWR from St John's Road to Shanklin began operations in 1864 and went on to Ventnor in 1866. Ryde to Newport followed in 1875 and Sandown to Newport, after some vicissitudes at Shide and Pan Lane, by 1880. 1880 saw the joint LBSC/LSW lines opened from Ryde Pier to St John's Road. The Bembridge branch followed in 1882 and the Freshwater line in 1889. Last of all the Newport, Godshill & St Lawrence, later part of the IWCR, got through to Ventnor Town by a beautiful run along a shelf in the Undercliff in 1900 after pausing at St Lawrence in 1897. This was all—the odd ideas like lines up the Back of the Wight through Chale and even more sensible ones like a line to Totland Bay, were all in the discard—and no more lines were seriously thought of. And indeed, in those far off seemingly golden days, ideas of truncation were equally remote. To have imagined London Underground stock on Lake Bank would have been an absurd fantasy.

None the less, electrification was often thought of and a consulting engineer's report of 1909 is in the possession of the authors. This suggested complete electrification of all the Island lines with a central power station of 4,000 KW at Newport with immediate extensions of the lines to

[1] One of them indeed carried the Island name of *Newport* when she was in yellow paint, one of many Brighton engines with Isle of Wight names, e.g. the E5 0-6-2 tank *Freshwater*.

Rails in the Isle of Wight

Seaview from Ryde, to Osborne and East Cowes from Newport and from Freshwater to Totland Bay. Further extensions were foreseen and the doubling of the busiest lines. The operation suggested was for motor passenger cars with trailers as required. The entire cost of the electrification of the existing system was estimated at £310,000 and the total cost to include buying out the existing stockholders was put at £1,200,000. Today it looks a bargain. But the trouble has always been to marry the demands of a large summer traffic, most of it on Saturdays, with a thin, indeed almost negligible, winter need.

A totally different picture could be painted if the Isle of Wight tunnel had ever been built. For years the Ordnance Survey maps had the line of the 'Proposed Tunnel' marked on them between the Lymington branch of the LSWR and the FYN between Yarmouth and Freshwater. A bill was passed through Parliament as early as 1901—and it was no doubt the prospect of a tunnel which excited the Great Central. In 1901 it was estimated that the entire project of 7½ miles of railway with a 2¼-mile single line tunnel—without electrification—would cost £535,000. This like the estimate for electrifying the Island railways looks like a bargain today but the matter died when World War I began. If the tunnel had ever been built, the Island would have been totally altered, with Western Wight, which today is still largely unspoiled, one vast slatternly holiday resort, fed by through trains from the mainland, Newport a big diesel depot, all utterly changed, and for the worse.

This then was how the railways of the Isle of Wight looked on the eve of amalgamation on January 1, 1923—except that the Freshwater Railway, for ever recalcitrant, declined to come in voluntarily and had to be compulsorily absorbed. Their earlier aspect before our first-hand knowledge began is rather harder to portray. Up to World War I the train services were infrequent, certainly compared with the prodigious services of the 1930s, slow though not much slower than between the wars, uncomfortable and dear. 'Parliamentary' third-class fares were hard to come by as only certain trains carried them; second-class on the other more convenient trains cost twice as much as the unattainable third.[1] On the other hand to be fair, there were almost innumerable excursions in the summer. However in 1913 the plunge was taken by Russell Willmott, the new General Manager of the IWCR, and third-class was made available on all trains.

[1] For example the Board of the Cowes & Newport Railway resolved on June 10, 1862 to run eight trains each way on week-days with two regular trains and one excursion each way on Sundays. Of these the 'Parliamentary trains' were to be the first each day from Cowes and the last each day from Newport.

35. An early 1920's scene with IWR 2–4–0T *Wroxall* arriving at Brading with a train for Ventnor

36. *Ventnor* resting in Ventnor yard under the slopes of St Boniface Down. Photo 1920

37 and 38. Two views of *Bonchurch*, the upper with old four-wheeled stock near Ryde St John's Road in 1919 and the *lower*, emerging from Ventnor tunnel with the 1922 cut-down chimney

CHAPTER 2

The Southern Railway
First Phase 1923-1928

Under the Railways Act of 1921, the Southern Railway Co. was formed on January 1, 1923 though the Isle of Wight and Isle of Wight Central Railways had in fact been absorbed on the day before by the London & South Western. The Freshwater Yarmouth & Newport Railway stood out against the act until August 1, 1923 when it was compulsorily included in the Southern.

The first job was to improve the train services on the 'Main Line' between Ryde Pier Head and Ventnor and the SR decided to put in a half hourly train service during the summer season of 1924. In order to do this a passing loop-line was necessary at Wroxall, and this with a new down platform, and passenger overbridge were built in time that year. The unexpected station restaurant at Wroxall, the only one on the IWR, continued to provide good meals as before.

The station buildings at Ryde Pier Head which were deplorably primitive were entirely rebuilt and electric luggage cranes for the loading and unloading of the steamers were installed in place of the old steam cranes. Later the electric tramcars working between the Pier Head and Ryde Esplanade were found to be worn out and were scrapped in 1927 and two Drewry petrol cars were substituted, two of the original trailer cars being kept to work with them, one of them the famous carved and decorated 'Grapes' car. In this first period the station buildings at Ventnor were also rebuilt.

It was soon clear that many further improvements were needed in the next few years for an efficient railway service to be built up. Good timekeeping on the old Isle of Wight Railway, when more frequent trains were in operation, with single line running between Ryde St John's Road and Ventnor was impossible if either the down or the up trains were running late, which was often the fault of the boats from the mainland, even when several passing places were available on the route.

The first thing to do therefore was to convert the two parallel single lines from St John's

35

Road, one going to Ventnor and the other to Newport as far as Smallbrook to double track, by the provision of a scissors crossing and a new signal box named Smallbrook Junction. This improvement was brought into use in 1926. It was so constructed that the box could be closed and the two lines could revert to parallel single lines during the thin services of winter.

Then in order to help train punctuality further, as holiday traffic in the summer began to increase, the Southern decided to double the line between Brading and Sandown, a distance of $2\frac{1}{4}$ miles. A cutting and several bridges were rebuilt to make this possible. The section was opened on June 23, 1927.

Then on the other Island routes the main lines of the IWCR, consisting of pretty flimsy flat-bottomed rails, were lifted and relaid with chaired track sent from the mainland. Newport station buildings were partially rebuilt and the whole running layout altered and relaid with chaired track and new signals. By 1926 it was possible to start a half hourly passenger service between Cowes and Newport, the trains going alternately to Ryde Pier Head or Sandown to give an hourly service to them, but in order to give a regular hourly service between Ryde, Newport and Cowes, a passing loop line and a new island platform and station building were constructed at Haven Street and the old passing places at Ashey and Whippingham were relegated to the duty of a wagon layby.

Push-and-pull trains were introduced on the branch between Merstone Junction and Ventnor where the Town station was more realistically renamed Ventnor West.

The through service from Ryde to Freshwater run by the IWCR had been discontinued in 1913 and was not reintroduced at this stage but from 1923 all Freshwater trains came into the main station at Newport. A very necessary relaying of track on the Freshwater branch between Yarmouth and Freshwater was made with chaired rail and the Town Gate viaduct at Newport and the Calbourne viaduct were strengthened.

Cheap Tickets which the Island railways had had in many varieties before the war were reintroduced by the Southern, to be available every day, and became so popular that an all-Island Weekly Season Ticket was issued at 7s 6d third and 10s 6d first-class, which embraced the 32 stations and $55\frac{1}{2}$ miles of route. The number of these issued was considerable, reaching over 35,000 per season in the mid-thirties.

In the meantime many changes were being made in the Locomotive, Carriage and Wagon stock and in order to meet the Southern plans, fresh plant had to be sent over from the mainland.

Early in 1923, two LSWR 0-4-4 tank engines of class O2 designed by William Adams in the late eighties for working on branch lines, were sent to Eastleigh works and equipped with Westinghouse air brakes and sent to the Island on the main deck of the Admiralty floating crane from Portsmouth, and landed at Ryde Pier Head. Still lettered 'LSWR' and numbered 206 and 211, they were intended for working on the Ryde Pier Head—Ventnor services, and turned out to be exactly right with their extra power and flexible wheelbase for working all over the Island as a standard type of locomotive in the future, when the civil engineer had strengthened the track and bridges on the other routes. The second pair, Nos W21 and W22, was sent over in 1924 to St Helen's Wharf in parts and re-erected in the Island by fitters sent over from Eastleigh.

The Southern Railway's Southampton Docks had in the meantime acquired a 150-ton floating crane and this was to be used in the future for transferring locomotives and rolling stock to the Island. The vehicles were secured on the crane's main deck and with three tugs in attendance would make a three-hour journey from Southampton Docks to Medina Wharf where the unloading took place.

39. In 1923 when the first two O2 class tank engines had just arrived they worked for a time in their LSWR colours

40. By 1924 most of the old Island engines that were to be kept for any length of time were repainted in the Southern 'sage-green'. Here is No. W14 *Shanklin*; her appearance is confused by her having acquired *Ryde's* boiler

41. No. W23 in Shanklin station in 1925 with a train of old IWR Metropolitan eight-wheeled stock. Pictu
of these coaches are rare, though many of the bodies survive to this day on the sea-wall at St Helens

42. With her new green paint and elegant Wheeler and Hurst chimney, No. W8 looked a sharp lit
engine in 1924

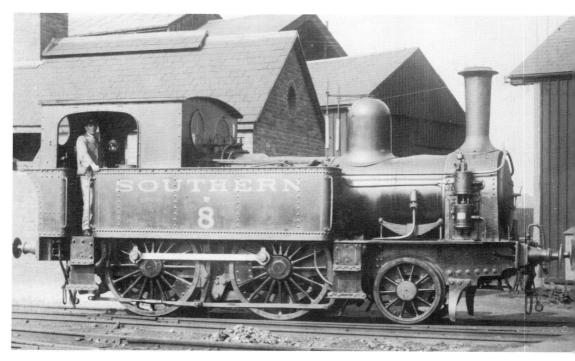

The Southern Railway—First Phase

Of the eighteen Island locomotives surviving at the time of amalgamation in 1923 many were showing signs of wear after performing many years of tough service, and as there were at least eight different classes it was decided that they should during the next few years be replaced by a minimum number of types from the mainland. So, although the IWR *Bonchurch* and the IWCR No. 6 were powerful engines and in fair condition, it was agreed they should be withdrawn and broken up owing to the difficulty of obtaining spares for them in the future. No. 6 was given a trial on the Ryde—Ventnor line but it didn't go at all well; she lost time consistently and this sealed her fate. Nevertheless the others with only a few years of service to look forward to were repainted in the current Southern 'sage-green'. *Sandown* after running 1,374,751 miles in her 59 years went to the scrap heap at once, but *Shanklin*, *Ventnor* and the other IWR tanks were repainted green and given numbers for the first time in their lives. No. 4 of the Isle of Wight Central was not repainted and was cut up in 1925, Nos 5, 6 and 7 went the next year and the 'Terrier' No. 9 in 1927. But in 1924 the Southern take-over of the Island engines was still at its maximum. The arrival of the O2 tanks, released some of the IWR 2–4–0s for the Central lines and *Shanklin* and *Brading* were early allocated. In 1923–4 before these were repainted it was possible to see engaging combinations at Newport such as double-headed trains led by IWR and IWC locomotives and in the station at Newport, for the only time in history, the three liveries of the Island railways at one and the same time.

But by the end of the summer of 1928 only *Ryde* and *Wroxall* of the IWR, Nos 8, 10, 11, 12 of the IWCR and Nos 1 and 2 of the FYNR remained in service. The IWR 2–4–0 tanks had given good service, for *Ventnor* had logged 1,298,310 miles, and *Brading* 1,212,753 miles; *Shanklin* recorded 1,492,121 miles and *Bonchurch* 1,326,067 in her short life.

The intention was to have two classes only to work the services in the future—and finally to have only one class in the Island; the ex-LSWR O2 class 0–4–4 tank engines were earmarked for the heavier duties and the ex-LBSCR A1 or A1x class ('Terrier') 0–6–0 tanks for the smaller branch lines where weight restrictions precluded the working of the O2s. In all, since the first arrivals in 1923, twenty 'O2s' and three 'Terriers' were imported up to the outbreak of World War II and three more O2s were sent over after it, a few arriving each year. In the event, another class, the E1 0–6–0 tanks, were sent over also but this belongs to a later chapter.

In 1923 many of the Island coaches were out of date, some were lit by electricity, some by coal-gas and others by oil; none were steam heated. They were a run-down ramshackle lot. It was decided that in the next six years, ten or twelve coaches would be transferred from the mainland each year, fitted with Westinghouse brakes, electric lighting and steam heating.

To start with, a standard coach for the Ryde–Ventnor service was evolved on the mainland by converting several former London Chatham & Dover Railway six-wheeled suburban coaches into four-wheelers to ease them on the sharper curves in the Island where they would be made up into four-car close-coupled set-trains. They were then in good condition being teak-built throughout, and were expected to last for several years.

The three sets of ex-LSWR low roofed bogie coaches, made up into sets of three were sent over for the Cowes–Ryde and Cowes–Sandown services. The remaining passenger services were to be covered by some four-wheeled four-car close-coupled sets which had their origin on the LB & SCR.

At the amalgamation there were 580 wagons on the Island of various types, many in a poor condition; so during the next five years, many were broken up and replacements of standard ex-LBSC 10-ton open and covered vans were sent over periodically in a barge via St Helen's Quay or were assembled from parts sent to the Island.

Rails in the Isle of Wight

A word might be said here of the Railway-owned ships which plied between the mainland and the Isle of Wight. The main service operated between Portsmouth Harbour and Ryde Pier Head, and in 1923 this was covered by five paddle steamers owned jointly by the LSWR and LB & SCR. They were the *Duchess of Fife, Duchess of Kent, Duchess of Norfolk, Duchess of Albany* and the *Princess Margaret* and all had been constructed between 1889 and 1911. They continued to work this service under the SR but with black-topped buff funnels instead of white, along with the addition of one new paddle steamer the *Shanklin* built in 1924.

In 1928 the *Duchess of Albany* and the *Princess Margaret* were replaced by two new paddle ships the *Portsdown* and the *Merstone*.

At the other end of the Island the steamer service between Lymington and Yarmouth was worked by the small LSWR paddle-steamers *Lymington* and *Solent* (II) built in 1893 and 1902. The Southern Railway added a third ship in 1927, another small paddle-steamer *Freshwater*.

The motor car traffic which was increasing by 1923 between the mainland and the Island, had been operated by the Lymington and Yarmouth route in towed barges and by the non-Railway boats of the Southampton, Isle of Wight and South of England Royal Mail Steam Packet Company via Southampton and Cowes, most of the motor-cars crossing by the latter route.

An examination was, therefore, made for a slipway to be made at Ryde with a view to a motor-car ferry service being instituted from there to Portsmouth, but it was found to be impracticable owing to tidal difficulties.

On further examination a satisfactory site for a car slipway was found in Wootton Creek at Fishbourne to the west of Ryde; this was built together with a landing point on the slipway at Broad Street in Portsmouth. Two double-ended double twin screw motor ships, with end gangways were built in 1927/8 for this vehicle ferry. They were named *Fishbourne* and *Wootton*.

The first five years of the Southern Railway in the Island was thus marked by steady if unexciting progress but all was not well on the mechanical side and in 1928 the General Manager of the Southern Railway asked one of us to go over and take charge.

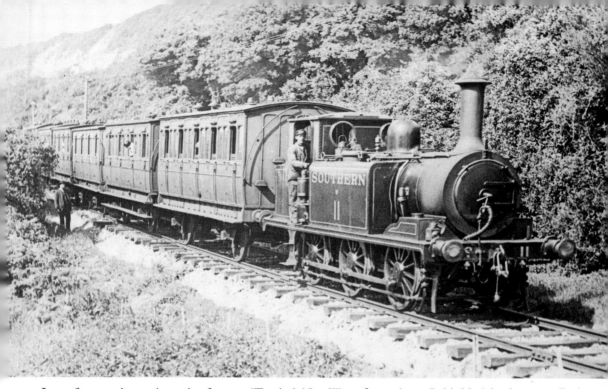

43. Just after amalgamation; the famous 'Terrier' No. W11, formerly a Gold Medal winner at Paris, near Ventnor West with a crop of aged coaches

44. Soon after the O2 tanks arrived to work the old IWR main line, a couple of IWR tanks were released to support the IWC services. This picture shows *Brading* in Southern green at Newport in 1924

45. 'The first of the many'; O2 tank No. W19 formerly LSWR No. 206, with an IWR coach and some sixty-year-ol
second-hand IWR coaches from the North London Railway leaving St John's Road

46. First painting style before the locomotives were named; O2 tank No. W28 with Drummond boile
at Newport in 1926

CHAPTER 3

The Southern Railway Second Phase 1928-1934

THE NARRATIVE OF A. B. MACLEOD

In 1928 it came about that I was transferred from Waterloo to the Isle of Wight to take charge of the Locomotive, Carriage and Wagon Department. I had never been there before, even for a holiday and my previous nine years on the railway after coming out of the Army had been spent in the LB & SCR locomotive works at Brighton and with the running of locomotives on the LBSC and SECR sections of the Southern Railway since the amalgamation.

My first close sight of the Island then was from the paddle-steamer *Duchess of Norfolk* approaching Ryde on a misty autumn day. Everything looked wet and depressing.

My predecessor met me and after a hurried lunch seemed anxious to leave as soon as possible for the mainland. We did, however, go down to the headquarters of the Department which was at Ryde St John's Road, where I was warned that I must remember that I was an 'Overner' and not an Islander and would have difficulty with the staff, some of whom were alleged to have Bolshevik tendencies. I was introduced to the Locomotive, Carriage and Wagon foremen and taken round the works. We then returned to Ryde Pier Head and I said goodbye and wished him luck. This was returned, and so I found myself in charge, with an independent command at the age of twenty-eight.

Back then to St John's Road works for a look round, with an introduction to each member of the staff. I was a proper new boy and said I must go and get some 'digs'. The locomotive foreman gave me some addresses to go to but asked if I would first settle an urgent problem which had not been solved and was causing trouble. 'You see, it's like this,' he said, 'the leading engine fitter caught an owl in the erecting shop this morning and won't let it go because he wants to sell it to a taxidermist for stuffing.' 'Why didn't you let it go?' I said. 'Well, you see the fitter is a Bolshevik and very difficult,' he replied. 'Where's the bird?' I said. 'Oh, it's now in the oil stores,' he said. There was the unfortunate Barn owl flopping about in one of the oil trays. The fitter was sent for and advised about cruelty to birds, also that the Southern Railway did not pay him to catch owls in the company's time and that he must try and clean off the oil with paraffin and put the bird in a nearby wood. That settled that, and the owl was able to fly away. Such was my introduction to the 'Garden Isle'.

Next day was a Saturday so I spent the week-end inspecting some of the equipment and rode on the footplate to Ventnor and back on one of the O2 class engines.

The running shed at Ryde St John's Road was deplorable. It consisted of a corrugated iron barn with a curved roof which just gave cover to four engines, standing over the inspection pits. There was a covered loading bank for a coal stage. This was all sandwiched into the goods yard, which made operations difficult.

The locomotive yard and running shed at Newport, however, were better and situated behind the goods yard, adjacent to the old IWCR workshops. The running shed had a louvred roof, which did allow the fumes and smoke from the engines to escape, unlike Ryde. Newport shed could also provide cover for at least eight engines over the pits; the coaling was carried out from an inadequate covered coal stage or out in the yard.

My first journey on the Newport–Freshwater line was eventful as some of the telegraph lines came adrift from the insulators and became wrapped round the 'Terrier's' chimney and this caused some delay in untangling the wires.

Within a week I had explored all the routes of the Island Railways and my first impressions were that with the existing equipment the best was certainly being done by the staff under great difficulty. The scenery from the trains was enchanting and I much looked forward to having a car and exploring the road system at a later date. I knew that when I had got the hang of things I would be very happy here—and so I was.

The main repair works was at Ryde St John's Road and consisted of a large brick building of two bays, with numerous corrugated iron and wooden sheds attached and a large water cistern embossed 1870, but any extensions to the buildings or the South Yard were restricted because of the Small Brook on one side and the station on the other; at flood times the brook would overflow and flood the station and goods yard.

At Newport the repair shop was at the north end of the running shed and adjacent to the main stores which supplied all the railway departments.

The supervisory staff consisted of three people, a locomotive foreman at Ryde and at Newport and a carriage and wagon foreman at Ryde. The Ryde office, under a head clerk, was a small building joined to the oil store in the yard at the north end of the shops near the road bridge which spanned the end of the station.

Having seen all these things my enthusiasm was somewhat damped and I realized it would be some time before I could go exploring the Island countryside—indeed, until I had made out a report on the position and had been up to Waterloo to see my chief.

There was, however, some humour in the situation as the landlady at my 'digs' on the evening of my arrival told me the century-old joke that the Isle of Wight was noted for 'Cowes you can't milk', for 'Newport you can't bottle', for 'Freshwater you can't drink', 'Ryde where you walk', 'Needles you can't thread' and 'Lake without water'.

The first thing was to know the staff. They certainly met me half-way and through the following years were wholeheartedly co-operative. The so-called Bolshevism completely evaporated.

The most colourful characters were the three supervisors and the head clerk. I feel I must mention them by name. At Ryde was Robert Sweetman, the locomotive foreman, Albert Brading, the carriage and wagon foreman, with a surname of unquestioned local origin, and

and 48. In 1925, painting in a better style began with a change of shade in the green paint. Then in 1929 all engines began to carry names, the lettering and lining out were improved and the numbers removed to the bunkers. Here are No. W13 *Ryde* with a train of Brighton four-wheelers at Brading and No. 27 *Merstone* with a Drummond boiler

49. The *East to West Through Train* later 'The Tourist' the first non-stopping through train since 19
started in 1932 to run between Shanklin and Freshwater. Here it is leaving Sandown behind E1 0–6–0
No. W3 *Ryde*

50. A locomotive failure of the Bembridge branch was dealt with by double-heading, the relief engine
No. W16 *Wroxall* piloting down as far as Brading

Sam Prismall, the head clerk. At Newport there was William Glassey, the locomotive foreman.

At the first joint meeting I held with them, I found the Newport representative was inclined to disagree with the Ryde point of view; however, it soon appeared that he was rather jealous of the fact that the old IWR line was earning more receipts than the old IWCR line. He called the former rather sarcastically the 'Élite' Section with its holiday resorts at Sandown, Shanklin, Ventnor and Bembridge.

It also transpired that none of these people had ever been allowed a week-end off duty but were always 'on call' in case of mishaps in the mechanical side of working the trains, both in winter and summer.

This was soon put right by an arrangement being set up to allow any of the four to have every third week-end 'off' as well as regular weekly evenings 'off call', which would enable them to leave the Island periodically in addition to their normal annual leave. The boss would also take his turn of being 'on call'. From that moment things improved.

The foremen were told to wear bowler hats instead of cloth caps as in the past, which in those days was deemed to give them greater authority over the staff under their control. However, I never did get Bill Glassey to wear a bowler hat more than once as he said it hurt his head but he did, as a concession wear a trilby hat sometimes in place of the cap, which increased his prestige at Newport.

In the winter of 1928, my first in the Island, I was rung up one evening and advised that there had been a derailment at Wroxall of the 8.43 p.m. train ex Ventnor and would I come. A few minutes later Bob Sweetman phoned me to say that several coaches were tangled up at Wroxall owing to a broken gauge glass on W23.

We took the Ryde breakdown tool van up to Shanklin but as the single line was occupied to Wroxall, the van and engine had to stop there. We put some jacks and packing in Bob's bull-nosed Morris touring car and, with a fitter and mate, proceeded by road and found a 'right angle up'.

As W23 was entering the south end of the loop line at Wroxall a boiler gauge-glass burst, filling the cab with steam, the driver threw his coat over the broken gauge glass and endeavoured to shut the regulator and apply the emergency brake, while the fireman put on the handbrake but unfortunately the engine had passed the starting signal at 'Danger' and by then had gone two coach lengths beyond the north end of the loop before coming to a stand, splitting the points, which were set for the Down track and fouling the Down Home signal in the process. The fireman had by then been able to shut off the gauge cocks under the driver's coat.

The driver then, not fully realizing the position, released the brakes, reversed his engine and opened the regulator to set the train back into the Up platform.

The train was composed of two sets of four close-coupled ex-LCDR four-wheelers, six of which were still on the right road. You can imagine what happened then; the second coach spread-eagled at right angles and the first coach and W23 tried to go into the Down road, and as the train was close-coupled no couplings gave way and the movement came to a sudden halt. But this was not all the trouble as it transpired that the 8.43 p.m. train ex Ventnor was running late and in order not to delay the 8.20 p.m. train from Ryde Pier Head, which was normally due to cross the Up train at Shanklin, the signalman had advised Shanklin to let the Down train proceed with a view to crossing at Wroxall instead.

So while all this drama of W23 was going on, the Down train, with another O2 class engine, was pounding up Apse bank towards Wroxall and might have struck the wreckage as the Down Home signal had been lowered. The fireman of W23 saved the day by running down the bank and placing fog signals on the track and so stopped the train from Shanklin but it was quite a near thing.

Luckily there were no passengers in the first two coaches of the Up train and so no complaints were made except for bad jolting to the people in the last six coaches when the train finally stopped. The few passengers in both trains were sent forward by taxis, which had been summoned from Ventnor. The Down train was sent back empty to Shanklin and the breakdown van sent up. We had to cut through the long coupling links with the oxy-acetylene cutter in order to free the leading four-wheelers before effecting rerailment with the jacks. It took till 6.00 a.m. to clear the line and repair the points, and the mails, instead of going through to Ventnor on the 4.00 a.m. train from Pier Head, had to be transferred to a lorry at Shanklin.

A joint enquiry was held by the Traffic Superintendent at Newport and as a result there were some awards and some chastisements and the whole affair caused quite a stir on the railway. This was the worst derailment I can remember; thank goodness it was not raining.

My report on conditions was made to Waterloo and I was sent for and after explaining things I was told that the difficulties had been appreciated when the Directors' inspection took place in August 1923. Schemes were being got out for improvements which would include the Locomotive, Carriage and Wagon side, but in view of my report a commission would visit the Island.

As a result of this, in the next few years, much was done. Ryde St John's Road station was rebuilt and modernized with new signals, a new signal box was erected there after transfer from Waterloo Junction and the goods yard was remodelled. A new running shed was built on a new site behind the station, with a new coal stage, ashpits, etc. More up-to-date equipment was installed in Ryde workshops and these became the locomotive and wagon repair shops for the whole Island.

The old locomotive workshops at Newport were stripped and fitted up for carriage repair and painting so that the coaches would have regular touching up and varnishing as well as regular general repairs.

In 1925 the locomotive colour had been changed from the LSWR 'sage green', which had been used by the SR since 1923, to the coach green, a deeper mid-green shade similar to the old Great Central Railway locomotive colour, the lining remaining the same as before, a white line with square panel corners bordered by a black band.

Then in 1928/9 the new policy of locomotive naming was introduced in the Island. Brass nameplates were cast in Eastleigh Works and sent over for fitting. The names selected were all connected with places in the Island.

These were as follows:

W1 *Medina*	W22 *Brading*
W2 *Freshwater*	W23 *Totland*
W3 *Carisbrooke*	W24 *Calbourne*
W4 *Bembridge*	W25 *Godshill*
W10 *Cowes*	W26 *Whitwell*
W11 *Newport*	W27 *Merstone*
W12 *Ventnor*	W28 *Ashey*
W13 *Ryde*	W29 *Alverstone*
W16 *Wroxall*	W30 *Shorwell*
W19 *Osborne*	W31 *Chale*
W20 *Shanklin*	W32 *Bonchurch*
W21 *Sandown*	

The nameplates were fitted to the side tanks a third of the way up from the bottom under the word SOUTHERN which was reduced in size while the locomotive number was transferred from the tank side to the bunker. The first engine to be named in the Island, in this scheme, was W19 *Osborne*, although W4 was already named when sent over to replace ex-IWCR W8 which was broken up in 1929.

It is interesting to note that thirteen of these names had once been carried by LBSCR locomotives of various classes, when it was the practice at Brighton to name all engines.

There were level-crossing collisions from time to time as when a train from Cowes collided with a lorry full of cement and came into Newport pure white from buffer beam to tail light. Later a train on the Freshwater Branch collided with a tractor on a crossing and needless to say the tractor suffered most and the tractor driver luckily jumped off in time. The driver of the 'Terrier' engine concerned was alleged not to have sounded his whistle. Instructions were, therefore, issued for all locomotive whistles to be sounded when approaching all crossings, entering tunnels as well as when entering and leaving stations.

This order caused numerous complaints from residents, especially near Ryde Esplanade Tunnel: also a lady passenger nearly had a fit when the ex-IWR *Wroxall* sounded its shrill Beyer Peacock whistle under the road bridge at Ryde St John's Road when leaving for the Pier. Caledonian Railway type organ-pipe (hooter) whistles, similar to that which had already been fitted to many of the Isle of Wight Central engines by Bill Glassey some years before, were now fitted to all engines and this much mellower note ended complaints, although numerous 'wags' said that they had heard that the steamers were now running on the railway.

I can remember one glorious Sunday in 1929 when Bob Sweetman insisted that I should borrow his bull-nosed Morris and go over the Downs from Brading to Newport, and as I sat on the highest point on Mersley Down I heard an O2 on a Sandown-Cowes train sound the new whistle at Alverstone, Newchurch and Horringford; it gave me quite a thrill.

By the way, this spot gives you a wonderful view, looking over a blue Spithead to Hampshire on one side and to St Boniface Down, above Ventnor on the other, with the villages all laid out like a map under your nose.

Still in 1929 I remember that whenever shunting was required in Ryde Works yard, an engine had to be in steam for this work and in order to curtail the expense of lighting up a locomotive for this purpose, I suggested that the staff should move any wagons, one at a time with pinch bars, but naturally this was not popular and meant much effort with a slow result. In order to get over this problem an improvisation was made in the form of a small manual tractor, designed to move the wagons more easily. We built up a wooden chassis and platform on four small coupled wheels (14″ diameter) with a 5-foot wheelbase and two hand-wheels on a centre column and a two-speed gear box of 1 to 1 and 4 to 1 ratio, with a chain drive—thus *Midget* was born. In low gear 20 tons could be moved with little effort and this stopped the complaints.

At the beginning of 1930 I was given control of the traffic and commercial departments in addition to the locomotives and rolling stock; this meant transferring my headquarters to the Traffic Offices at Newport station. This was a nice airy office high up in the station building with a good view of Newport station and yard to the north. This had been the HQ of the IWCR and had been occupied by General Managers Leonard Conacher and Russell Wilmott, important names of the past; it was most interesting to look through the archives and relics they had left behind.

My chief clerk was a pleasant man named Beazley who had been at Newport for many years. He helped me a lot with the traffic and commercial problems as, of course, many new things had to be learned, such as making up one's own timetables, graphically with the aid of a most helpful traffic clerk named Brimson, as well as Sam Prismall who had now transferred from Ryde Works: they made a most efficient team and helped to keep me 'on the rails'.

It was most interesting working out the summer timetable and then trying it out on my O-gauge layout with clockwork engines at my home near Ryde to see if the connections could be kept. The model railway was pregrouping Caledonian and Highland Railways but it did not matter, the names of the stations were temporarily changed; Perth became Newport I remember and Inverness became Freshwater.

After the 1929 summer season, the increase in receipts was so great that a half-hourly service on Saturdays was insufficient to cope with the increasing number of visitors to Sandown, Shanklin and Ventnor. A new timetable was therefore produced giving a Saturday service of three trains each way hourly over this route in 1930.

The problem was whether there was enough rolling stock to carry this out and so after a most detailed examination by a most helpful traffic assistant, Ivor Marshall who came down from Waterloo, it was decided to ask for more locomotives and coaches to be sent over from the mainland.

Two more O2 class tank engines W17 *Seaview* and W18 *Ningwood* and another A1x class W9 *Fishbourne* and several ex-LCDR teak bogie coaches duly arrived on the floating crane.

These coaches were in excellent condition and the whole of the SR stock of them came over to the Island in the next few years as a standard coach for the main lines in the Island. All the bogie coaches which were already in the Island were taken into Newport carriage shops and converted to give the greatest seating capacity; one of these was the old Midland Railway coach which had been purchased by the IWCR for railcar use in 1907. This had already been taken off her six-wheel bogies but we fitted her out in fine style.

This was the end of the four-wheeled coach era on the Ryde–Ventnor section and only bogie coaches were to be used there in the future except for the long four-wheeled luggage vans which were attached to all the trains next to the engine from Ventnor. This was to facilitate the transfer of luggage to steamers at Ryde Pier Head. Wheeled cages were used for this and were hauled by Lister petrol Auto-tractors.

Attached to my office at Newport was a traffic inspector who would generally keep an eye on the everyday working of the signalmen, guards, shunters and so on. While I was in the Island, I had at least four different ones, all excellent fellows, who worked round the mainland operating Divisions, with a period on the Island. The inspector would look after the train working on summer Saturdays at Newport, while I controlled the operations at Ryde Pier Head. I much enjoyed this experience; it certainly kept me busy, with the locomotive and train movements in and out of the station.

I noticed on these Saturdays that frequently the operations were keenly watched by a schoolboy. I spoke to him one day and found he was very keen on railways. He lived in Ryde and his name was Gordon Nicholson. I employed him as a volunteer, unpaid, unofficial runner, who helped me a great deal in checking in the trains, finding out which engines wanted coal or had to go to depot at St John's Road owing to a minor defect, or even to be replaced by a standby engine. He much enjoyed doing this and felt he was 'with it'. His ambition was to become a railway man, but his father had other views; however, after Mr Nicholson had talked the matter over with me, he realized his son would not be happy in any other career. Mr Nicholson went to Waterloo to see the Chief Mechanical Engineer, and in due course Gordon became a pupil in Eastleigh Locomotive Works.

In later years, amongst other positions, he took charge of the Island Railways from 1943 to 1946 and is now in 1967 an Assistant General Manager at Waterloo.

The Pier Head on these days was a mass of scurrying people, going to and from the steamers, some walking, some on the trams, but the majority were on the trains. As many as 36,000 passenger were dealt with on the trains on these summer Saturdays.

At this time the story was told of the staff at the Pier Head being unable to persuade an old lady to leave the train. She said, indignantly, that she certainly was not going to change as the Station Master at Shanklin had assured her that this was the Waterloo train.

There was a certain amount of special traffic on the railway up to 1930. The Ashey Races were a great event—about 2,000 passengers going from Ryde and 1,000 from Newport in special trains which used a siding leading to the racecourse grandstand. Unfortunately, just after the 1930 races the grandstand was burned down and horse-racing in the Island has not been resumed since then. It was rumoured that a tramp had sheltered under the grandstand and had lit a fire to keep warm and went to sleep, suddenly waking up to find the grandstand alight and decided to make himself scarce.

The other big event was the Cowes Regatta week in August, a heavy special traffic being handled from Newport. On the Friday night of the Illuminations and Fireworks, the late freight trains from Medina Wharf were cancelled and special through trains were run from all parts of the Island to and from Cowes, about 5,000 passengers being dealt with during the evening. Bill Glassey always liked to come with me to this event at Cowes because it was a big day for Newport and I suspect he also much enjoyed what he called 'Darjeeling tea' at the Station Refreshment Room during the evening, and during the extension period that was granted on that night well after the usual closing time. I enjoyed this 'tea' also as it was well laced with whisky. This was a great favourite with Bill who, surprisingly for a Scot, always stipulated 'John Jamieson' brand.

Bill Glassey was a great character. He had been a regular driver on the Caledonian Railway and drove No. 774, a Dunalastair II class 4–4–0 Express locomotive for several years, stationed at Polmadie Shed in Glasgow. He gravitated to the Lancashire, Derbyshire and East Coast Railway as Shed Foreman at Langwith Junction and finally came to the IWCR as locomotive foreman. He told me that on many occasions in the old days, when the engine crews did not turn up for duty, that he had driven and fired the engine of the booked passenger service to Ryde and back so that there would not be a complaint from Russell Wilmott, the General Manager.

Bill was always partial to his drop of whisky in those days which had singularly little effect on him, but I think he was nearly teetotal the last time I saw him when he visited us in Wimbledon. He was very knowledgeable on roses and used to visit the Royal Horticultural Society's Gardens at Wisley. I always had a great regard for him.

As the holiday traffic was still growing, two large paddle-steamers were ordered from the Fairfield Shipping and Engineering Company of Govan, for the Portsmouth and Ryde services. These two vessels, named *Southsea* and *Whippingham* were delivered in the summer of 1930 and were the first paddle steamers of modern design, a feature was the continuation of the promenade deck right up to the bow. They were a great asset to the route, as they could carry 1,100 passengers, and were capable of a speed of 16 knots. They were also found to be suitable for local cruises, and the *Southsea* was frequently used for excursions 'Round the Island' and up Southampton Water to view the liners in the Docks.

Also in 1930, with the continued growth of motor car traffic another double-ended ferry, the *Hilsea* was built by Denny Brothers of Dumbarton, similar to the *Wootton*, and put to work on the Portsmouth to Fishbourne service.

An important occasion for the Isle of Wight section of the Southern Railway was the Directors' Inspection which was due to take place in the spring of 1931. One of the places they were anxious to see was the new Medina Wharf where a new deep water quay 500 ft long had been authorized to replace the old and rather primitive wooden wharf.

A large area behind the quay and running the full length of it, was to be used as a storage for the coal required for the Isle of Wight. Two electrically operated transporter cranes would span this area, each with two 30 cwt. grabs and enable the colliers to be discharged more expeditiously than in the past and reduce demurrage to a minimum. The coal wagons could be loaded as required and sent to the coal factors at the various stations, notably those at Ventnor whose storage was carved out of the chalk cliffs of the station yard, for road delivery to the consumers. Electric capstans were also to be installed to shunt wagons on the quay.

This coal traffic was fairly heavy and amounted to over 100,000 tons discharged each year. Waterborne traffic, other than minerals, was dealt with at St Helens Quay, where improvements were also being made.

I can vividly remember meeting the Chairman, Brigadier-General the Honourable Evelyn Baring, the other Directors and Sir Herbert Walker, the General Manager and his chief officers at Ryde Pier Head, then going down the pier on the Drewry tram and on by motor coach to inspect the Fishbourne Car Ferry slip in Wootton Creek, then to Ryde St John's Road station, works and running shed, St Helens Quay and Brading station. From there they went by ordinary train to Ventnor while I went home to put on a dinner jacket and get to the Royal Marine Hotel at Ventnor by 7.30 p.m. to dine with them. After dinner I was questioned by the majority of the Directors and officers and I hoped got by.

Next day a special train, consisting of a four-wheeled saloon and a four-wheeled two-coach pull-and-push set with an A1x, took the Directors from Ventnor West to Newport, Cowes, Medina Wharf and Freshwater, where a Southern-Vectis bus took all of us to Yarmouth Pier where the steamer for Lymington was waiting. I remember thinking on the Pier that all would be over in another few minutes, when the Chief Mechanical Engineer, R. E. L. Maunsell, took me aside and said in a very stern voice that he was very dissatisfied with the train lighting, as apparently on the previous evening, when going by the ordinary train from Brading, upon entering Ventnor Tunnel, the electric lights were switched on in the compartment and after a split second were reduced to a faint glow. Several of the Directors then shamed him by referring to the 'Fairy Lights' in the Island trains. I asked him why he had not mentioned this last night at Ventnor. He replied, 'I didn't want to spoil your evening.' He continued, 'I have authorized expenditure on equipment for electric train lighting and it is not being properly used, see about it at once.'

I felt very small, as the PS *Freshwater* left Yarmouth Pier. When I got back to Newport and sent for the carriage electrician, his plea was that this particular set train had been changed at the last minute and was now due for battery recharging. Nevertheless, I gave him a piece of my mind and clear instructions for the future. I was greatly relieved to hear later on that the inspection had been quite successful and that I still could carry on in my job. The CME came down soon after this and was satisfied with how things were going. He always barked at you but he was very fair and always backed you up.

I shall always have most pleasant recollections of Major-General G. S. Szlumper, who when he was Assistant General Manager, was Chairman of the Southern-Vectis Omnibus board on which I also sat. In the spring of the previous year he kindly invited my wife and me to accompany them to Glasgow to attend the launching of the *Southsea* by Mrs Szlumper. I remember we travelled by the *Royal Scot* Anglo-Scottish Express of the London Midland & Scottish Railway who had just put on two new trains for this service. They were of a new order of comfort as the first class compartments, with only four seats, all had different décor and were adjacent to their own special Dining Car and so obviated a long 'trek' down the train for meals.

Szlumper later became General Manager and I will always be grateful to him for the kindly advice he readily gave me at all times.

But some inspections were not always successful. I recollect receiving a message one morning that the Chief Operating Officer and his wife were travelling from Bournemouth that afternoon and would like to divert from the normal route to Waterloo and go via Yarmouth, Newport and Ryde and then proceed to Waterloo via Portsmouth. They would like tea served between Ningwood and Ryde Esplanade in the saloon which could be attached to the rear of the ordinary service train, and would I please arrange for this to be done and to meet them at Yarmouth Pier.

You can just imagine the 'flap' that went on. The saloon was dusted out and bread and butter and fancy cakes were ordered through the Newport Refreshment Room, also a teapot, cups, saucers and plates as well. I think a special tray and a new kettle were bought in the town and a primus stove was borrowed for my traffic inspector to boil the water between Freshwater and Ningwood in a cubby-hole at the end of the saloon. I won't swear that this was the only meal ever served on an Island train but it must have been one of very few indeed.

This saloon was a four-wheeler ex-LBSCR and rode like most four-wheelers do. The VIPs duly arrived and I accompanied them in the saloon. All went well until we reached Ningwood, when the inspector brought in the tea which was poured out, but before it could be drunk, we were running down the 1 in 57 gradient on to Calbourne Viaduct and half the tea shot out of the cups and on to the table, saturating the table-cloth. By perseverance, however, and by only pouring half-cups, some tea was consumed before Newport over this switchback line, every rail joint being clearly felt in the saloon by the passengers and the crockery. On arrival at Newport, the saloon was detached and shunted to the far side of the Island platform to be attached later to the Cowes–Ryde train, but before this could take place a Cowes–Sandown train was due. This train normally took a number of schoolboys back to Sandown from Newport, and as we stood at the adjacent platform these schoolboys arrived for their train. They immediately made a bee-line for the saloon, which was a strange coach to them. 'Coo, look, a Dining Car', they shouted, seeing the remains of our tea: then several of them proceeded to press their noses on the saloon windows and blow loud 'raspberries'. The inspector and I rushed out of the saloon and made arrangements for the Medina Wharf engine (old FYNR No. 1) which was standing in the nearby goods sidings to uncouple and shunt us round in amongst the coal wagons as expeditiously as possible.

The Chief Officer kept murmuring, 'Most regrettable, MacLeod, most regrettable'. The tea was cleared away into the cubby hole and the rest of our journey to Ryde Esplanade was uneventful. The Chief Officer's wife got out there and said she would come on by the tram, while we were inspecting the Pier Head Station. Just before the steamer was due to leave a very red and harassed Chief Officer's wife came up to us and complained that I did not provide an attendant to look after the Ladies' Room at the Esplanade station. I replied that the expense of providing one had not been granted. The VIP asked what had happened and his wife replied that her penny had stuck in the slot and the door would not open and although she tried for

53

some time she had in the end to use another penny in another slot. The Chief Officer murmured 'Very unfortunate, MacLeod, very unfortunate; see that an attendant is there in the future' and she was.

My day usually consisted of visiting Ryde Works first in the morning and then when the day's programme had been agreed with Bob Sweetman and Albert Brading, I would go on to my office at Newport and deal with traffic and commercial matters.

The old office at Ryde Works was being used by Sweetman combined with a large amount of stores which had increased greatly, so this office was turned into an extra store and part of an IWR Metropolitan eight-wheeled coach body which had ended its useful running life was laid down in the yard at the north end of the works and after stripping became quite a good office for him with much more room.

At this period I had hired a bathing tent at Seaview for the season and my wife and I often had a picnic lunch there and a swim as well. The beach there was very popular and more and more visitors came there for the day, usually on small ferry boats from Gosport, which were festooned with life-belts and were known as the 'Sixpenny-Sick'. At high tide the 'Overners' would hire deck chairs and sit at the water's edge and would goggle at the big liners which frequently passed, never dreaming that about fifteen minutes afterwards the wash from these vessels would reach the beach and upset them into the sea. This frequently happened and was a source of much amusement to the Islanders. I mentioned all this one day to Sweetman and he said his family wanted him to take them to Seaview sometime and he said he would go the coming Sunday afternoon. On Monday morning when I saw him he seemed rather quieter than usual so I asked how he'd got on. He said he was disgusted with what he saw. 'There the were, Master, all rind off, like meat in the butcher's shop, but (this ominously) time will tell' I often wonder what he would have said about the sights on some Continental beaches today. Strait-laced or not, he was an excellent foreman and engineer and a very good friend to me and we had very many happy occasions wrestling with and solving the mechanical problem which arose from time to time.

Albert Brading, the carriage and wagon foreman, was also a very proficient cabinet make who had produced some lovely work. I shall always be in his debt for the rudiments of carpenter ing which he taught me. He was most reliable and only had to be told about a thing once and was done. Albert's first wife was alive during my first few years in the Island and she must have been a great deal older than he was and deaf as well. She would follow him to work, a few paces behind, and would hang about outside the works all the time he was in there, standing on the bridge at St John's Road, waiting for him to come home to lunch or knock off at night. If you asked Albert whether his wife didn't trust him, he would just smile and say nothing there may have been a story behind this, but we never found out. He had the nicest nature of any man I ever knew.

Spithead was always a source of great interest and hardly a day passed without some liner passing or during the summer yacht-racing of many classes. I always liked to see the big 'J' class, especially the King's Yacht *Britannia* with her huge spinaker set for running before the wind. The schooners and three-masters always looked well, with all their sails set. I recollect the arrival of the new Norddeutscher-Lloyd 50,000 ton liners, *Europa* and *Bremen*, steaming up and anchoring off Cowes and sometimes one could hear the band playing on board when the wind was in the right direction. I was told how luxurious they were and that Claridge Hotel in London was a mere second class inn in comparison, and that the illuminated 'name between the two funnels was lit at night by a mere 1,200 lamp bulbs.

54

51. *Ryde* at Bembridge after she had acquired a Drummond chimney from the SR as well as *Shanklin*'s boiler. The second coach was the old IWC rail motor coach and the third the old Midland twelve-wheeler rebuilt

52. Group of 'Terriers'. No. W9 *Fishbourne* brought over by the SR and Nos. W10 *Cowes* and W12 *Ventnor* from the IWCR. Nos W9 and W10 have the standard Marsh A1X chimneys

53. W11, ex LBSC No. 40 *Brighton*, later IWCR, in Freshwater station about 1927. The leading carriage is of LSWR origin, ex IWCR, with a close-coupled set of LBSC Billinton four-wheeled carriages.

54. The floating crane attended by three tugs, off Medina Wharf

55. Former LDCR coaches being put ashore in 1932

56. The E1 tanks arrive, 1932. *Medina* in the air with *Ryde* and *Yarmouth* waiting

I also remember seeing during these years the British R–100 and the German 'Graf Zeppelin' airships serenely traversing Spithead along the Hampshire coast; also the arrival in Cowes Road of the German 'Dornier Do-X', twelve-engined flying boat, which was the largest aeroplane in the world at that time.

But as in 1929, the big event of 1931 was another Schneider Trophy contest. This was flown on a triangular course of 217 land miles, with turning points at East Cowes, West Wittering and opposite the entrance of Bembridge Harbour. Large chequered pylons were erected round the masts of three destroyers to act as markers.

During the race all shipping was halted. The SR erected a grandstand and seating on the end of Ryde Pier, and visitors to see the race were provided with a ten-minute service pull-and-push train between Ryde Esplanade and the Pier Head. The 'Terrier' W3 *Carisbrooke* worked the train.

The entrants were the British and the Italians, the former being able to compete and defend their title as winners of the 1929 race only by the generous gift by Lady Houston, a most colourful figure in the air world at that time, of £100,000 to the Royal Aero Club.

But for some reason the Italians withdrew at the last minute and Britain was the winner. The British team, however, with their Vickers Supermarine S.6B Seaplanes fitted with Rolls-Royce engines proceeded to fly the course and break all previous records. To see the little blue and silver monoplanes with their huge floats flash by low over the sea on the 'golden' day was a sight I shall never forget. The speeds were round the 400 m.p.h. mark, which was 'going some' in 1931.

At the end of that year, W16 *Wroxall* of the old IWR came in for general repairs and we fitted her with a short Drummond chimney and the commodious cab which came from IWCR 2–4–0 tank No. W8 which we had kept when this engine was broken up in 1929; this cab gave better protection to the engine crew.

In looking at the freight services at the end of 1931 it was found that there had been little improvement in the loads hauled since the amalgamation, especially between Medina Wharf and Newport. At the former, owing to restrictions in weight on the old jetty, only A1x class and the FYNR saddle tank W1 were permitted to work there. The new quay was nearly ready and when completed would allow heavier engines to be used. W1 and the three A1x class with 14″ cylinders could only haul twenty-five loaded wagons of coal from the wharf to Newport and in view of the restricted working from the wharf owing to passenger services on the single line between Cowes and Newport, this was found to be inadequate.

As the A1x class ('Terriers') had given such a satisfactory account of themselves, it was agreed to transfer from the mainland three ex-LBSCR Stroudley's E1 class 0–6–0 tank shunting engines, which were virtually an enlarged A1x class. Three of the E1 class were given general repairs in Eastleigh Works, fitted with modern Marsh boilers, with Ramsbottom safety valves and Drummond chimneys as already fitted to the O2 class, which would then bring these engines within the Island loading gauge of $12'—3\frac{9}{16}''$—the mainland loading gauge being $13'—1''$. The engines selected were old No. 136 *Brindisi*, No. 152 *Hungary* and No. 154 *Madrid*; they were repainted in passenger green colours and named at Eastleigh—W1 *Medina* W2 *Yarmouth* and W3 *Ryde*. These engines, with more bogie coaches, arrived at Medina Wharf on the floating crane on June 1, 1932.

The old *Ryde* (W13) which had worked the first IWR train from Ryde St John's Road to Shanklin in 1864 had now travelled 1,556,846 miles in her 68 years on the Island railways. Towards the end of her life a short Drummond chimney had been fitted and a modified cab, rather changing her appearance. Her last days were spent working on the Freshwater branch. She was now withdrawn and was replaced by the new *Ryde* (E1). There seemed to be a chance at one time that the engine might be preserved but this was not to be[1] and the best that could be done was to alter her back to as near the original condition as possible in 1933 and repaint her in grey with black and white lining in the IWR style to be photographed from all angles. She finally went back to the mainland on the floating crane in 1934, to be broken up at Eastleigh in August 1940. Another veteran which had now come to the end of her life was the old FYNR No. 1 which for her last three years of service had borne the name *Medina*. This Manning Wardle saddle tank engine had been built in 1902 and was therefore the youngest engine to have worked in the Island, except for the IWCR railcar engine which hardly counts. No. 1 belonged originally to Pauling & Co. who were the contractors for the construction of the Great Central & Great Western Railways joint line and at that time bore the name *Northolt*. In 1913 she was sold to the FYNR and was first employed on passenger services from Newport to Freshwater but soon after the amalgamation she became the regular engine at Medina Wharf. After an Island life of nineteen years, she finally returned to the mainland to be broken up at Eastleigh on June 1, 1932 when the new E1 *Medina* arrived to replace her.

A great amount of work was done on the locomotives and rolling stock during 1932–3. Complaints from the drivers were being received of cold wind blowing through the cabs, so to stop this, all engines were fitted with hinged cab doors, which were a great asset.

Then in order to improve the appearance of the whole stud of twenty-seven engines, I felt that a standard chimney had to be found. The majority of locomotives had LSWR Drummond chimneys and on visiting Eastleigh I found that the smaller Drummond chimneys used on his version of the Adams 0–4–0Ts (B4 class) in Southampton Docks would be suitable for the A1x class. These were fitted to the five of them which had either 13″ or 14″ cylinders, while the two remaining, *Carisbrooke* and *Fishbourne* which had lined-up 12″ cylinders kept the thinner copper-capped and Marsh cast-iron capped chimneys respectively.

During this period the standard painting of SOUTHERN on the O2 class tank sides had also been used on the A1xs and the two old IWR engines and looked far too large and out of proportion. So a reduced SOUTHERN was painted on the tank sides which suited the engines much better. By this time a pride in the locomotives' condition had been instilled into the staff and cleaning ceased to be a problem, so I decided to paint the wheels more carefully, and line them out. This paid off as I found that cleaners who are keen on their work, liked to clean lining and lettering as they can then see some result from their efforts. It was also possible to have all the locomotives allocated to regular crews, and they in turn kept their cab 'fronts' polished.

With the advent of the three E1/class engines W1, W2 and W3 the seven A1x class were numbered in sequence from W8 to W14. W2 *Freshwater* became W8 (this engine now lost its Drummond boiler and was rebuilt as a standard A1x), W3 *Carisbrooke* became W13, and W4 *Bembridge* became W14.

The Civil Engineer's Department had found that several of the piles on Ryde Pier Head required renewal, and as this was an extensive operation, the SR decided to provide an additional platform road in the station on the west side making four platform faces available for traffic. This work was completed before the summer services of 1933.

As the Ryde–Ventnor route was still finding an increase in its summer passengers, a further revision of the timetables was made during 1933, with a view to providing for an increased service for summer Saturdays when the fourth platform at the Pier Head would be available;

[1] My fellow author tells me that he contributed a hard-earned fiver to this good cause which he never saw again.

57. The fourth and last E1, No. W4 *Wroxall* which arrived in 1933

58. One of the authors on the footplate of *Totland* in 1931

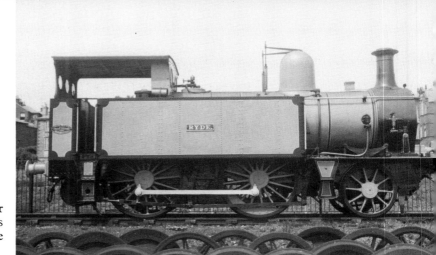

59. *Ryde* restored for preservation, but alas the campaign to save her failed

60. W20 *Shanklin* in full pre-war livery with big bunker introduced by A. B. MacLeod

61. Sailing barge passing through the drawbridge at Newport

this ultimately gave three trains from Ryde to Ventnor, one to Sandown, and one to Newport and Cowes in each direction each hour from 10.00 a.m. to 6.00 p.m.; this service of five trains an hour into and out of Ryde Pier Head was augmented in later summers to a maximum of six trains an hour and was the highest ever attained.

In order that the O2 class engines, which worked these services could remain longer in traffic without returning to depot for coaling, we decided to enlarge their bunkers from $1\frac{1}{2}$ tons capacity to 3 tons. An experimental 'Great Western' style one was first fitted to W19 *Osborne*, but the extra height of the coal stack masked part of the rear spectacles. A new design was therefore made avoiding this difficulty, which became the standard. The plan was to fit the ten Adams-boilered O2s (W17–W26) stationed at Ryde first, and follow with the six Drummond-boilered O2s (W27–W32) stationed at Newport, later. No. W26 *Whitwell* was in fact the first engine to be turned out with the new standard bunker.

By now, in mid-1933, the new quay at Medina Wharf was finished, so tests could be made with the E1 class on the coal trains from there. These were most successful, the previous limit of twenty-five loaded wagons was first increased to thirty and later to forty, the permissible number of empties back to the Wharf now became forty-five wagons. To work with these trains several of the ex-LSWR 10-ton combined road and goods brake vans were rebuilt with a 'veranda' at each end and fitted with sanding gear to prevent the wheels picking up when the hand brake was fully applied.

We kept the wagon shop at Ryde works very busy at this time. The old dumb-buffered ballast wagons were worn out so several new 10-ton drop-sided ballast wagons were turned out and painted in red oxide. The old IWR 12-ton open wagons were refurbished for internal yard use at either Ryde or Newport for ashes, clinkers, and such-like. Then the two old water tank-wagons and an ex-IWR brake van were rebuilt and fitted up as a weed-killing train, and the ex-IWR long-wheelbase carriage-truck was strengthened, fitted with a well for use as a boiler truck for the conveyance of the O2 class engine boilers.

Some old Island Railways' wagons were broken down to the underframes at Newport, and were then placed touching each other in rows between the coaling roads there and when covered with old sleepers made a raised coal stacking ground for locomotives, as the existing stage was found to be too small for modern requirements. This eased the difficulties of the coaling gang by not having to fill the engine bunkers by shovelling off the ground.

At this time inwards fish traffic was being loaded at Ryde Pier Head into passenger luggage vans and complaints were received when these luggage compartments were not thoroughly cleaned out, that the passengers' luggage smelt of fish. Several of the ex-LBSCR Westinghouse-fitted 10-ton covered vans which were working in the Island were fitted up for FISH TRAFFIC ONLY and so cured this problem.

During the summer of 1932 the transport of passengers' luggage was becoming a continuous anxiety, as the margin of time between the boat arrivals at the Pier Head and the departure of the Island trains was small and if the boats were late, the trains had to leave on time owing to the reaction over the single lines which would be caused by late running. So a campaign of sending 'Passengers' Luggage in Advance' was launched which considerably eased the position but it became necessary to select a number of Westinghouse-fitted covered goods vans and allocate them to PLA traffic, the outward luggage being loaded into these vans on Saturday afternoons, so that in the evening a train of PLA vans could be run from Shanklin picking up loaded vehicles at Sandown en route to the Pier Head. The luggage was then sent over to Portsmouth in the late hours of Saturday night.

Rails in the Isle of Wight

The rebuilding of the Wharf at St Helens had now been completed with a new layout, deep water quays, and rebuilt steam cranes; it thus became a useful port for waterborne cargoes other than coal, although continuous dredging was still required in Bembridge Harbour.

The popularity of the weekly season tickets was increasing, it was decided therefore in the summer of 1932 to introduce some through trains, which would give the passengers a much quicker journey between the most popular places in the Island. Six coaches were labelled *East and West Through Train* and ran during the week (except on Saturdays when traffic prevented it) from Shanklin to Freshwater, in each direction calling only at Sandown, Merstone Junction, Newport, Carisbrooke and Yarmouth. An E1 class engine worked this train between Shanklin and Newport, and an A1x on to Freshwater. The old IWCR railcar, which had been rebuilt several years before as an open third saloon with wooden slat seats and fitted with second bogie (when the 0–4–0 engine unit had been removed in 1911) was now rebuilt into third-class corridor observation coach to run in the through train.

After the trying experience of numerous inspections carried out in the old four-wheeled saloon, I went to the mainland to find a bogie replacement, and after some searching the ex-LB & SCR invalid saloon was allocated to me for the Island and was sent over with the floating crane on its next trip, and this vehicle, with several more ex-LCDR bogie coaches arrived in 1933, with a fourth E1 class engine, W4 *Wroxall* (ex-LB & SCR No. 131 *Gournay*). The last Beyer Peacock 2–4–0 of the Isle of Wight Railway, W16 *Wroxall*, was therefore withdrawn and returned to the mainland for breaking up, after running 1,350,674 miles in the Island during her life of sixty-one years.

Owing to the immediate popularity of the *East and West Through Train*, seven additional through trains were run in the 1933 summer service between the Ryde-Ventnor line and the Freshwater branch. The original through train now started from Ventnor with an accelerated timing and became the first named train, each coach carrying a board with 'The *Tourist*' in gold on a red background. A second through fast train was also included in the programme between Ryde Pier Head and Freshwater, the first for twenty years.

Apart from running the Island trains, there were other problems which occupied much of one's attention.

One of these was a continued disappearance of stores, which were sent almost daily from the Newport General Stores Depot to Ryde St John's Road, either for the works or stations on the Ryde-Ventnor line. These parcels never arrived at St John's Road, although they were put in the guard's van on the regular Newport-Ryde passenger train.

A detective sergeant came over from the Portsmouth Railway Police Headquarters and discussed the matter with me, and a watch was kept, but without result. One day, when I was at the St John's Road works office, a distraught woman asked to see me and implored me to intervene on her behalf, as she was Mrs X, the wife of one of the Newport guards. It appeared she had applied for her usual annual holiday free ticket to the mainland, and it had been refused by the booking office at St John's Road where she had collected it in previous years. I said I would look into the matter and she could come and see me the next day. It turned out upon investigation that a Mrs X had already received her one annual holiday free ticket for that year. So when Mrs X called back at the works office next day and was told that she had already had her free holiday ticket she became very abusive about her husband, and swore she had never had it. The application forms were examined, and it transpired that there were two Mrs X's, one living at Newport and one at Ryde. The Ryde woman, who had come to see me was not married to guard X and on hearing of the proof, she admitted that guard X lived with her at Ryde without benefit of clergy and had never told her about his lawful wife at Newport, only 8½ miles away. She then became 'a woman scorned' and said she had lent him her greenhouse for a workshop, but did not know what he did inside, but none the less would I send someone up to look at what he had in there.

I got in touch with Railway Police Headquarters in Portsmouth, and the detective sergeant came over again and went up to see the 'workshop' where he found of course the missing stores, piled high in the greenhouse, not only consumables, like soap, clothes, oil, and so on for the stations, but also such things as hammers, chisels, spanners and emery paper, which had been ordered for the Ryde works.

The guard was convicted of theft and dismissed the service and in the final interview 'came clean' and admitted he was the regular guard on the train which normally brought the stores and on arrival at St John's Road nipped out of his van and hid the parcels under the signal box and then when booking off at night took them up to his mistress's house. He had no idea what he intended to do with these things, but could not resist collecting them. He was not penitent, and considered he suffered from ill luck.

But stolen stores were not the only problem, as wagon tarpaulins also seemed to 'walk away' and on the six-monthly count, many were always missing. The Railway police came over in force and made searches near the lines all over the system. Several were found covering boats, chicken houses or sheds with leaky roofs. One rather blatant case of theft was a bed quilt hanging on a clothes' line near Mill Hill station, which on closer inspection turned out to be a number of 1st class carriage antimacassars sewn together. Attention had been drawn to it as it had been flying out like a white flag in a high wind, and had been seen from a train by one of my staff.

Talking of wind, we certainly had our share of high winds and rough seas and on occasions were cut off from the mainland for several days at a time, the paddle-steamers finding it impossible to land passengers at Ryde Pier Head in an on-shore gale. Their sponsons would fill in very rough weather and make them very hard to handle.

On occasion we also had heavy continuous rain, which caused flooding between Newport and Sandown and in Ryde Esplanade tunnel, making it impassable for trains. One notable event a little later on was the great thunderstorm of August 7, 1937 when the Esplanade tunnel was flooded and all evening trains had to be stopped at St John's Road; buses were put on to carry passengers to Esplanade station and a train, isolated on the pier kept things moving with a shuttle service.

Heavy rain I remember also caused a landslide at the south end of St Lawrence tunnel, which closed the branch from Merstone Junction to Ventnor West, and took many hours to clear. Luckily we never had a heavy snowfall during my years in the Island; only one lay with more than a few inches. On this occasion we fitted out the old IWR tank *Wroxall* with brooms attached to the guard irons to sweep snow off the rail head. I did experimentally fit one of the O2 class with a wooden snow plough, under the front buffer beam but that seemed to frighten the snow, as it never came again, and the plough was never put to the test.

One interesting item cropped up, when I was approached by the Ryde Repertory Theatre Company to advise them on the railway 'props' required to perform the 'Ghost Train' at the local theatre. We had a lot of fun, evolving the train noises required to represent the passing of the ghostly express outside what looked very like one of our SR waiting room-cum-booking offices. We even made up a model starting signal with a massive arm and counter weight, which when pulled from the invisible signal box, clanged most realistically. In fact, the signal

63

was so satisfactory, that it ended up at Fishbourne, where it was erected to control the car on to the Fishbourne–Portsmouth ferry.

Another change from routine was the inspection of all the stations for the prizes for 'Best Kept Stations' given by the Directors. My wife was a great help here, by inspecting the 'LADIES' and making pertinent comments where necessary.

I can recollect one stupid derailment about that time which took place at Bembridge on the last train of the day. Upon arrival of the train from Brading the engine was uncoupled before running round via the little turntable; the guard who lived near the station, passed the locomotive in the dark and shouted 'Good night' to the driver on his way off the platform, the driver mistook what he heard for 'All Right' and gave the engine steam and went straight into the turntable pit, as the fireman although on the ground at the time, had not yet set the turntable for the engine to run on. The Ryde breakdown van was sent for, the electric 'staff' had to be taken to Brading in a taxi to let the breakdown train into the branch. It took all night to get the engine back on the road, and thence to the works for minor repairs, and a fresh engine was turned out in the morning to work the first train on the branch.

In 1934 as additional bogie coaches had arrived in the Island the two original IWCR short bogie coaches which had been built by the Lancaster Carriage & Wagon Co. in 1889 and had before 1913 been used on a through service between Ryde Pier and Freshwater during the summer season, became spare from main line work. These were taken into the works for rearrangement of seating to suit the Brading–Bembridge services. They were attached to either of the 12″ cylinder A1x's (W9 and W13) and worked on the branch for the next few years.

In this year during the summer service no less than fifteen through trains were run on weekdays and on Sundays two through trains were added from Ventnor West to Freshwater.

I did not however have the pleasure of seeing all this come about, as a vacancy at Waterloo arose in the Locomotive Running Department and I was appointed Assistant Western Divisional Locomotive Running Superintendent, and so officially left the Island in May 1934. would now have to learn the old LSWR system and although there would be compensation such as visits to the Lynton & Barnstaple Railway in North Devon, which came in the Division I was very sad at going.

I had enjoyed a wonderful experience, which I shall never forget; with a regular staff of 475 persons it was possible to exercise the personal touch, and try to know something about all of them, and it was gratifying to be able to help them sometimes with their personal problems.

Although still an 'Overner' I had at the end been accepted by them as being an Island Railwayman. During my six years, I had met many splendid people, both in the Island as well as on the railway, several of them I have been fortunate to keep as friends.

On the railway side nearly all of them have passed on, with the exception of Sam Prismall my old locomotive running clerk, who did so much for me on the administration side of the job; he has now retired and is still doing yeoman service as secretary to a society of railway pensioners in the Island.

I will always remember that it was on Newport station in 1930, that I first had the pleasure of meeting my fellow author Peter Allen who like me loved the Isle of Wight and its fascinating railways.

CHAPTER 4

To World War II and After

In time for the summer service of 1934 the Divisional Engineer strengthened the bridges on the Freshwater line, and put in a larger turntable at Bembridge, so it now became possible for the O2 class engines to work over these branches. This easing of the engine restrictions was a great benefit as 'the *Tourist*' through train could now be hauled all the way by an O2. This train had been accelerated, leaving Ventnor at 9.55 a.m., calling only at Wroxall, Shanklin, Sandown, Newport and Yarmouth, arriving at Freshwater at 11.12 a.m. The return from Freshwater was at 5.20 p.m., arriving at Ventnor at 6.46 p.m. During one summer week no fewer than 2,700 passengers travelled by this train. As well as the third-class corridor observation coach, the ex-LBSCR invalid saloon was also included, which had a first-class observation compartment as well as a coupé, and a large open third section. The 'picture-windows' were much appreciated, as they gave excellent views of the scenery.

More bogie coaches arrived from the mainland during 1935, some of which once belonged to the LBSCR, with their long brass hand-rails as the whole of the stock of ex-LCDR bogie coaches had already been transferred to the Island.

So the service continued on a high level and the numbers of passengers continued to build up, reaching a new record in 1937. To meet this growth more stock was brought over in 1936, more bogie coaches and four more O2 tanks, W14 *Fishbourne*, W15 *Cowes*, W16 *Ventnor* and W33 *Bembridge*. The opening of all lines to these engines made four of the 'Terriers' redundant so W9 (the second 'Terrier' to carry this number) and W10 and W12 of the original IWC stock and W14—a Southern import—went back to the mainland to be used on branch lines or broken up. This left only three 'Terriers' out of the eight which served in the Island at one time or another, of which two W8 and W11 were old Island engines, the other being No. W13, a Southern introduction. In 1936 there were thus 27 locomotives in the Island together with 85 bogie coaches, 50 other coaches or vans and 607 wagons.

In 1938 the last Drummond boiler temporarily disappeared when O2 class W30 *Shorwell* on receiving a general repair had hers replaced by one of the Adams pattern, so that by then all the O2 class had the latter type of boiler as well as the large coal bunkers, though later the Drummond type boiler returned. In 1938 also, *Midget* the four-wheeled manual tractor used in Ryde Works yard was withdrawn for scrapping.

So to 1939 as the storm clouds of World War II were gathering. It is opportune to mention here the additions which took place in the Southern Isle of Wight fleet during this period. The *Duchess of Kent* needed replacement after thirty-six years in service, so another 'paddler' was ordered from Denny Brothers. Thus the *Sandown* slightly smaller than the *Southsea* and built to accommodate 900 passengers, arrived on the service in 1934 and with her cruiser stern was a most handsome vessel. She was followed by a sister ship the *Ryde* built by the same firm and delivered in the spring of 1937. The *Sandown* stayed in service until the summer of 1966 when she was sold, while the *Ryde* was withdrawn in 1969 and moved to Binfield on the Medina in 1970.

An incident occurred at Portsmouth Harbour during this period, when an old lady passenger, with her bag, was found on a seat overlooking the steamer berth having remained there for several hours, while three steamers had departed for the Island; when a member of the staff asked where she wanted to go, she replied 'I have seen steamers leaving with *Shanklin*, *Southsea*, and *Merstone* on them, I am waiting for one with *Newport* on it.'

At the other end of the Island the *Freshwater* was the mainstay of the Lymington and Yarmouth service, but as she had been built in 1927 and was not equipped for carrying motor traffic, something had to be done. At this time the cars were carried in barges and were loaded and unloaded at slipways at either end, and after being towed across the Solent by the old paddler of that name or by the hired tug *Jumsey*.

This method of car ferrying was not satisfactory, so in 1937 the SR ordered from Denny Brothers a double-ended car ferry boat, not unlike the *Fishbourne* of the Portsmouth and Fishbourne service. The new ferry, delivered in 1938, was named *Lymington* and was equipped with the new Voith-Schneider type of propulsion; the Voith-Schneider propellor consists of a number of feathering blades revolving on a wheel lying on its side. One of these is installed at each end of the ship, and gives great manoeuvrability, the ferry being able to move sideways or turn in its own length, in consequence it was soon nicknamed the 'Crab' by the passengers.

The Isle of Wight was in the front line throughout World War II from the Battle of Britain until the liberation of France. After the phony war period and the disasters of 1940 restrictions were put on casual visitors to the Island, though those with business or relatives there could pass after scrutiny. In 1940–4 there were no summer train services in the Island and unneeded coaching stock was given a coat of grey protective paint and parked in suitable sidings. On the other hand a considerable local traffic developed with workers going from all parts of the Island to Cowes to work in the shipyards and aircraft plants there. There was also the development of export traffic to the mainland of tomatoes which started after the loss of the Channel Islands in 1940. On the other hand the cement mills between Cowes and Newport were closed in 1944 when the Cement Marketing Board supplied all the Island needs from the mainland.

As G. H. R. Gardener, who was Acting Assistant for the Isle of Wight in the early days of the War recalls:

'As the war progressed I found general maintenance a problem as materials were scarce, holes in wagon boards, for example, having to be covered with tinplate, so that later on (1947–8) much really heavy work was necessary to bring stock up to scratch.

62. A busy moment at Brading in 1937 with No. W15 *Cowes* on Ventnor train running in while the Ryde train waits on the left. The Bembridge branch engine is on the right

63. The building of a larger turntable at Bembridge enabled the O2 tanks to work the Bembridge branch. Here is *Cowes* being turned in 1937

64. The three Island classes at Newport just before World War II, O2 0–4–4T No. W27, A1x 0–6–0T No. W13 and E1 0–6–0T No. W4

65. W16 *Ventnor* at Ryde St John's Road following a collision that took place during wartime blackout conditions

To World War II and After

Before leaving the war years, however, we did find workers' traffic increased tremendously, large numbers travelling from all over the Island daily to Cowes, and it was one of my duties to be at Mill Hill and Cowes each night with my Area Inspector to see out the four or so trains that departed from Cowes from 4.45 p.m. onwards, a real feat of operating this, over single track, and thought was given to provision of a crossing loop somewhere near Medina Wharf and this would have been necessary if the war had continued much longer.'

The Isle of Wight ships gave a good account of themselves during the Second World War, especially in the evacuation of allied troops from Dunkirk in May 1940, when *Whippingham*, *Sandown* (equipped as a minesweeper and flak ship), *Freshwater* and the two car ferries *Fishbourne* and *Wootton* were there. *Whippingham* alone brought back 2,700 men. The Red Funnel fleet from Southampton were there too and lost the *Gracie Fields* by air attack. *Ryde* was requisitioned by the Royal Navy and employed on minesweeping. There were unfortunately two casualties in the fleet, the *Portsdown* on normal service was sunk by a mine off Southsea in September 1941 while the *Southsea*, also a minesweeper and flak ship, having distinguished herself by shooting down an enemy aircraft in November 1940, struck a mine while minesweeping off the Tyne in February 1941, and although beached was declared a total loss. The *Lorna Doone* of the Red Funnel service from Southampton also distinguished herself; when attacked by three Dornier bombers while on her minewseeping service, she shot down one, damaged a second and drove off the third. A BBC radio programme was produced in her honour.

During the intense preparations for D-Day in 1944 the regular boats *Merstone* and *Shanklin*, with the little *Solent* from Lymington, the standby boat, were requisitioned to ferry troops to the transports for France lying in Spithead, and civilian movements to the Island were restricted to travel on the car ferries to Fishbourne with connecting buses to Ryde. At one time too the Red Funnel Line hired the *Princess Helena* to the SR for the Ryde service.

The Isle of Wight was the British terminal of the first Pluto petrol pipeline to France which ran from Sandown Bay to Cherbourg; the petrol was pumped ashore from tankers off Ryde and piped along the railway in the bed of Small Brook to a collecting point in the woods near Brading whence it was pumped under the sea to France.

While the Island escaped the fearful blitzes to which Portsmouth and Southampton were subjected, there were numerous 'incidents'—Cowes, Medina Wharf and Ventnor being hit, the latter in the frequent sneak raids on the big radar station which stood so conspicuously on St Boniface Down and played its part in the warning system which made victory in the Battle of Britain possible. Newchurch station was hit by a stray bomb which closed the line for a time and there is a story of a train being machine-gunned on Ryde Pier. On April 7, 1940 a stick of bombs fell across Ryde and one fell on St John's Road yard, damaging No. W16, destroying one coach, damaging others and some wagons.

Again let us quote G. H. R. Gardener on this:

'Medina Wharf, that brings memories, the famous night of the heavy raid in 1942, and dive bombing at that. We had just previously had an important meeting with Wharf staff asking them to work on beyond the first alarm with special lighting, this being taken by the District Chief—Charles De Pury—and also attending was John Marchbank, the NUR General Secretary, all promises from staff being given for co-operation. On the night of the raid, hardly had our lights (specially screened) gone on, than the planes came over, and it was somewhat dicey for a time, the middle Transporter being burnt out, water pressure being very low, and our District representative, Dabney, being hit by flying shrapnel when attempting to screen him-

69

self under a wagon; we finally got him to hospital, but he had lost the use of one ear, and spent a week or so in Ryde being attended to from time to time by my wife. Also attending this affair was a person who shall be nameless who had previously been telling us of his doughty deeds as auxiliary in the London blitz, but we did not notice any special leadership on this occasion, he being extended full length, and doing much crawling to and fro, as were we all.

On the whole though, it can be said that, unlike its neighbouring cities on the mainland the Isle of Wight escaped the war lightly.

The arrangement whereby the railways of Britain were taken under Government Control on September 1, 1939—although the railway companies still continued in existence—under the Emergency Powers (Defence) Act of 1939 with a Railway Executive appointed to run them was intended to cease a year after the war ended but by this time political events had outstripped operational procedures. In the General Election campaign of July 1945 the Socialist party had committed itself to nationalization of the railways and this was confirmed in Parliament on November 19, 1945. The text of the Bill was published on November 28, 1946 and its second reading was moved by Mr Barnes, the Minister of Transport, on December 16th. Although the Minister paid a sincere tribute to the magnificent job done by the railways during the war, the Chancellor of the Exchequer, Mr Dalton in the ensuing debate chose to emit these ungenerous words:

'Let us look at the railway system now. It is in very poor shape. Partly that is due to the strain of six years war: partly, but not wholly. Those dingy railway stations, those miserable unprepossessing restaurants, all the out-of-date apparatus for sleeping and eating, make one ashamed as an Englishman when one is travelling abroad and sees how well the thing is done in Continental Europe, Western Europe, in Sweden and France. (An HON. MEMBER: "In Russia.") We must get our geography right. I said "Western Europe." Still more do we feel that if we go to America and Canada. One feels very much ashamed in Canada of this branch of private enterprise in the old country. That is one reason why the tourist traffic is not so easily attracted here. The railways are in very poor physical shape . . .
I am saying that this railway system of ours is a very poor bag of physical assets. The permanent way is badly worn. The rolling stock is in a state of great dilapidation. The railways are a disgrace to the country. The railway stations and their equipment are a disgrace to the country. (*Interruption*.) We are talking about the values of these things and I am saying that they are a pretty poor bag of physical assets.'

(Hansard)

Anything that the railway companies might do or seek to do in the immediate post-war period was with the certainty that they would be taken over by the State sooner or later. In the event, the Transport Bill received the Royal Assent on August 6, 1947 and British Railways came into being on January 1, 1948.

While the Southern lines in the Isle of Wight emerged from the war without substantial damage they were, unlike Britain's other railways, not badly run down though suffering from minimal wartime maintenance. The floating crane had spent the war on the Clyde and the locomotive stock was unchanged during the war; on VE Day it consisted of four E1 0-6-0 tanks, Nos W1 to W4, three A1x 'Terriers' Nos W8, W11 and W13, and twenty O2 0-4-4 tanks Nos W14 to W33. There were 112 bogie and nine other coaching vehicles and 555 wagons of various sorts.

The story of the immediate post-war train service in the Island is vividly told by Gordon

66. Post-war finery. No. W13 *Carisbrooke* after restoration to full-dress uniform in 1945 — polished brass and copper, malachite green, fully lined out wheels. She demolished austerity single-handed

66a. Inside Ryde shed

67. No. W8, formerly No. 2 of the FYN at the end of the war in un-lined black though with her yellow lettering shaded in green. Her original chimney has replaced the Drummond type

68. Ryde Pier where most of the Island traffic originates. This picture dates from the early fifties and shows P. *Ryde* and M.Vs *Brading* and *Southsea* with Red Funnel Line *Vecta* alongside and trains in No. 1 and No platforms

69. The start of an unsuccessful experiment. Class E4 0–6–2 tank SR No. 2510 being unloaded at Medina Wharf, February 1947

70. No. W11 shunting a train of chalk from Shide to Cement Mills just before World War II.

71. *Godshill* at Newport in 1948 with the official saloon then in occasional public service as an observation car. This view clearly shows the large MacLeod bunker which all the Island O2s acquired

72. New locomotive shed at Ryde

73. No. W31 *Chale* in full malachite-green lined-out paint, 1947

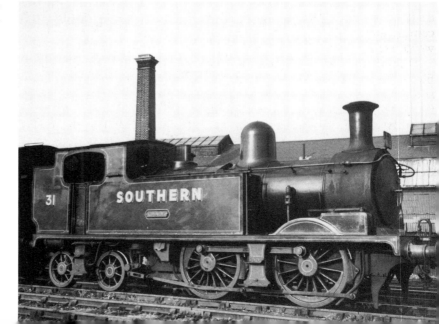

To World War II and After

Nicholson who was Acting Assistant for the Isle of Wight at the end of the war. His own words tell it best:

'The 1945 summer service was rather a triumph. I think the fleet was down to three—*Merstone, Shanklin,* both pretty well worn out, plus the *Ryde* which was refitted just in time. I persuaded Waterloo that there would be a devil of a rush to the Island if the war was over in the spring and got carte blanche to run the best train service we could within the Island to marry with a basic hourly service from London. Of course the Island rolling stock was in fair order and practically at pre-war strength—unlike the Mainland—and we put on what was almost a pre-war service, with three trains an hour on the Ventnor line, "the *Tourist*", with its two saloons, and so on. All this started on May 7, 1945, which was also VE Day! In the result both the ships and the trains carried an all-time record load that year, though I believe this was subsequently beaten on more than one occasion, and it led, at any rate as far as I was concerned, to a certain optimism during the 1945–6 winter, and I remember stating a case for doubling between Smallbrook and Brading and Sandown to Shanklin; and we even considered a diesel traction scheme which I recall turning down because of the seasonal load and the lack of night duties. It was not until a year or two later that the new fashion of branch line closures became all the rage.

We started painting the engines green again before the end of the war and lining them out properly, wheels and all. I remember the first was one of the "Terriers", No. W13. We also did up the ex-LSWR and FYN one (W8) as we found an old coppertop chimney somewhere in Ryde shops[1], dressed it up, and smacked it on in place of a perfectly good cast-iron one and picked out her black paint with Southern lettering shaded in malachite green.

It was in this sort of atmosphere that I got the E4 0–6–2 tank 2510 sent over. My idea at the time was that the best answer for the Ryde/Ventnor line was modern push-and-pull working on the French method of propelling almost any number of vehicles, and I wanted to see what a more powerful engine would do.

As you know, it was a failure. To the best of my recollection there were some footstep or buffer beam clearance difficulties which prevented its use on the Ventnor line and consequently it worked principally between Sandown and Cowes, where the extra power was of no particular service. I remember being extremely cross that the clearance trouble only came to light after it had arrived.

2510's arrival was preceded with some interesting speed tests with an O2 class and the ex-LBSC invalid saloon in which a Hallade speed recorder had been installed and I can remember coming down Apse Bank at well over 60, in an effort to convince the Engineer that his track would stand a good deal better than the overall speed restriction of 40. Halcyon days!

I think it was in the autumn of '45 that a film company came to the Island to make a travel film called "Chip off the Old Rock". Grasemann asked me to help them for some scenic shots and we went down the Ventnor West Branch one morning with the flat boat-truck in front of the engine and the saloon behind, mounted the cameras and the crew in front and went through St Lawrence tunnel, and they got a rather fine shot looking out to sea curving round as we turned down the Undercliff. What I had forgotten was that the Engineers were doing some work on the sea side of the tunnel and consequently had put down detonators in the tunnel to protect themselves and these went off with volcanic effect in pitch darkness and the Continuity girl, who was sitting in a deck chair, nearly had a heart attack.'

[1] This was in fact her own original chimney (with the tapered sides at the base) which had been used with the Drummond boiler.

One more o–4–4 tank, No. W34, came over in 1947 as one of the Island 'Terriers' W11 went back to the mainland, leaving Nos W8 and W13 *Carisbrooke* of this class and they went back in 1949. That year the last two o–4–4 tanks, Nos W35 and W36 were imported, bringing the total up to twenty-three for this class where it remained until they in turn began to be put to the torch in 1955. These last three O2s were named *Newport*, *Freshwater* and *Carisbrooke*.

Quoting G. H. R. Gardener again:

'I joined the RE's in late 1943 and enjoyed my time in the Middle East but that is another story; returning to the Island in December 1945, I at once had serious troubles on the maintenance side, eventually having broken axles on both O2 and A1x engines, our power position being so bad that one O2 loco was sent to Eastleigh for repair, and two others (W35 and W36) being later sent us to add strength, as summer traffic was now very heavy.

I well remember about 1948 being clapped and almost chaired out of the Chamber of Commerce meeting, when I announced increased services for the following summer, reintroduction of cheap day tickets and Holiday Runabouts, with also early morning cheaps, and the Chamber in those days was very critical; one thought at times if it were not for Transport in the Island (Rail and Vectis Bus Co.) the Chamber would have nothing to discuss.

Of derailments in past years, the two I recollect most were: a goods being propelled into the long siding at Shanklin, going well beyond the mark, with the result that the Brake and a number of wagons were thrown on to the main line, with heavy delays, the guard luckily escaping injury; and the summer Saturday morning when one of our O2 locos was derailed outside the shed at catch points, due to a misunderstanding between driver and shunter. When I was advised, I had thought of some four or five trains being cancelled, with the hold-up of perhaps two to three thousand travellers, but on checking my workings, I found to my great joy that the engine was only to work one short trip from Shanklin, then to shed spare. What a relief, and an almost impossible escape from great trouble, as the engine was right over on its side, and work of rerailing went on over the week-end, with help from Guildford, with special jacks and other equipment.'

For the summer services of 1965 which covered only a truncated system by then, the number of O2s was down to seventeen which barely provided for the intensive Saturday service and by the end of 1966, when the mileage of lines operated at last reached rock bottom, there were only ten of them in service with one further serviceable one set aside for preservation. Meanwhile, the E1 o–6–os were broken up, the first in 1956 and the last in 1960, leaving the O2s in sole charge.

Suggestions were heard in 1960 or thereabouts that BR class 2 2–6–2 tanks would be tried in the Island and ten were earmarked for conversion to Island standards, but by then it was really too late to think of anything except closures so the little O2 tanks carried on to the end of the steam service in 1966. Two were scheduled to stay in service for works trains, together with the o–6–o Hunslet diesel shunter brought over in October 1966, until the end of March 1967.

In 1946 the SR ordered from Denny Brothers two new vessels for the Isle of Wight service. They were named *Brading* and *Southsea* and were twin-screw Sulzer Diesel ships, electric-driven, and were the first screw-propelled motor-ships to be built for the route. They were delivered in 1948. They had a speed of 15 knots and are capable of carrying up to 1,400 passengers. A great innovation was also the provision of Radar equipment, which permitted the crossing over Spithead during fog. A sister ship *Shanklin* was added in 1951.

At the end of the war in 1945 the SR decided to order from Denny Brothers a further car

74. *Shorwell* on Ryde pier in the mid-sixties

75. E1 0–6–0 tank No. W1 in unlined black about 1955

76. *Bonchurch* on early morning train from Ryde emerging from Ventnor tunnel; *Chale* is on the left. 19

77. Coal train from Medina Wharf in 1961; locomotive is No. W31 *Chale*

78. Ryde to Cowes train running along the Medina, near the Wharf turnout, locomotive *Bonchurch*. 1961

79. Ryde Pier Head station in January 1965, locomotive *Sandown*

VENTNOR TRAIN

ESPLANADE
St JOHNS ROAD
BRADING
SANDOWN
SHANKLIN
WROXALL
VENTNOR

SHANKLIN

2

COWES TRAIN

ESPLANADE
St JOHNS ROAD
ASHEY
HAVEN STREET
NEWPORT
MILL HILL
COWES

PLEASE
SHOW
TICKETS

80. Off to Ventnor from No. 1 platform, Ryde Pier Head, 1964

81. Malachite green and top-class finish at the start of the BR era

82. Cowes–Ryde train emerging from Newport tunnel with *Chale* in 1965

ferry for the Lymington–Yarmouth service, which was delivered in 1948. The *Farringford* was a larger ship than the Voith-Schneider *Lymington*, fitted with four rudders and two English Electric diesel-electric motors each coupled to independent paddle wheels, giving speed of 10½ knots. A similar ship *Freshwater* was added in 1959 for this route. Two more motor ferries bigger than the original ones were added for the Portsmouth to Fishbourne route in 1961, a new *Fishbourne* and the *Camber Queen*.

Hardly were the post-war austerities overcome when economic problems appeared with ever-increasing severity. While the burgeoning of the affluent society brought more and more people to the Isle of Wight for summer holidays, putting an intense strain on the Ryde–Ventnor main line at week-ends, so the increase in private motoring reduced the need for the Island railways on the branch lines and in off-peak periods. As early as 1951 there was a strong rumour that British Railways wished to close the whole system down and as a first step proposals were made to close the alleged uneconomic branches. The Merstone–Ventnor West branch which was the last to be built was the first to go, being closed in September 1952. This and the proposals to close other branches aroused a lot of protest in the Island and this was not allayed when, at the special public enquiry held by the South Eastern Transport Users Consultative Committee in June 1953, it was asserted that the Railway had used some highly dubious figures to support its case. Nonetheless the Bembridge branch went in September 1953 and so did the Freshwater line. The Sandown–Newport line was given a two-year reprieve but in February 1956 it too was shut down. But enormous numbers of people would still flood through Ryde Pier Head on summer Saturdays—over 30,000 each way at the highest point, many of whom would swarm on to the trains which would leave packed to the roof. Five trains an hour would leave Ryde, four for the Ventnor line and one for Cowes, on the Saturday service. Yet British Railways with 2,800,000 passengers a year claimed that they could not make the Island railways pay, even when the lesser branches had been lopped off. As an example of high costs, heavy repairs had to be carried out to the Pier and the Pier Head station in the winter of 1963–4 costing some £250,000 as the result of which one running road was to be eliminated, which was done by the end of 1965.

Under the Beeching Plan of 1963, British Railways proposed to close the whole of the rest of the system at the end of 1965 in spite of pledges of long notice having been given in 1955 when the plan to shut the Sandown–Newport line was announced. This was the last straw, and at last produced an effective protest. The Minister of Transport held a hearing on the matter in June 1964 and a year later the decision was given that while the Ryde–Cowes line could be closed and Shanklin–Ventnor section of the main line could go also, the Minister accepted the argument that the rest of the main line was needed to prevent serious hardship, even though an expensive modernization would have to be carried out. This decision was accepted and British Railways set about providing a new service between Ryde Pier Head and Shanklin by means of a £500,000 third-rail electric system using redundant tube-railway stock bought from London Transport at scrap prices. The first car arrived for trial running to assess clearances on September 1, 1966.

Meanwhile the passenger service between Ryde and Cowes ended on February 20, 1966 (although goods trains continued to run intermittently as required) and between Shanklin and Ventnor on April 17th. At the end of the 1966 summer services, on September 17th, steam haulage ended on Ryde Pier except for an occasional work train and on the section between Ryde Esplanade and Shanklin on December 31, 1966. The new line with its electric trains reopened as planned in time for Easter 1967. Meanwhile, the Vectrail Society had hoped to reopen the Ryde–Cowes line with the aid of lightweight diesel railcars but this did not materialise. Instead, part of the line 20 years on has steam trains. (See Postscript, p94).

We asked our friend Hamilton Ellis to give us his observations on the end of steam on Ryde Pier.

Afterthoughts from Ryde Pier
by Hamilton Ellis
(September 1966)

If the end is not to be indeed heroic, surely decent things should go out like decent people, quietly and without fuss. Decent things include steam trains, which are now going out all over the world; and thus went out the steam trains on Ryde Pier in the Isle of Wight on Saturday, September 17, 1966.

Of course, trains were not going from the Pier entirely, nor were steam trains going immediately from the Island. They would continue south of the Esplanade for a little while longer, with possibly an odd work train up the Pier now and then, after which, for a while, the line to Shanklin would be like the Pier extension, apparently dead. Then the blue electric trains which once were red would come next summer, the whole thing being rather like the metamorphosis of a butterfly.

Standing on the planking of the Pier, on that last Saturday afternoon, it was hard to believe that this was not going on for ever. To be sure the trains looked more dirty. Over yonder the hovercraft came in and went out. In one moment one was proud that we had produced so ingenious an invention and not the Americans, nor the Germans, nor the Italians nor—God save the mark—the Japanese. In the next, as one of the things roared up the beach, one was reminded of Tacitus describing the Scots Army that opposed General Agricola, his father-in-law, near Stanley Junction: 'Shouting with terrible din, after the manner of barbarians . . .' Then as the appliance sat down on the beach to discharge its passengers, one waited for it to rise from its squat, wondering whether, like a turtle, it had left some eggs. Then between us and the hovercraft rumbled those old trains, the designer of whose engines had served the Kingdom of Sardinia in the Rissorgimento; and between the trains and us were those strange green trams—not so very old, and motor-driven at that—which nevertheless seem to have about them an aura of extreme age like a cœlocanth. One kept expecting one of them to come along towing the celebrated 'Grapes' car, that primeval ornate tram dating from the horse-drawn era which was at Ryde for so long and then went to Hull Museum. Behind us drove the occasional cautious motorist, well behaved, or an ill-behaved motor-scooterist, both new sorts of people on the Pier.

Latest memories always conjure earliest ones. My first experience of the Island and its railways belong to the nineteen-twenties, when the engines of the Isle of Wight, and the Isle of Wight Central Railways were still around and about, together with various people's cast-offs, such as that Stroudley 'Terrier' on the Freshwater line which had come at third-hand from the London and South Western; with Dugald Drummond's dome she looked like a North British Class R branch-line tank engine, apart from her original copper-capped chimney.

There were other Stroudley 'Terriers', of course, all on the Isle of Wight Central. Only the IWR had a standard engine, of the sort built for many lines about the world by Beyer Peacock and Company in the eighteen-sixties and 'seventies. The Southern Railway's first import had been that of Adams O2 tank engines, two of them, in 1923. We guessed at the time that

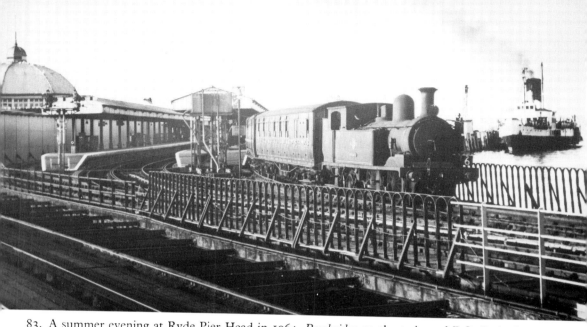

83. A summer evening at Ryde Pier Head in 1964. *Bembridge* on the train and P.S. *Ryde* alongside

84. *Ashey* at Ashey, October 1965, on train for Cowes

85. Early morning start down the Pier. *Bembridge* on the 6.55 a.m. train for Ventnor. 1961

86. *Freshwater* pulling out of Ventnor in 1965. The coal merchants' old caves in the chalk cliffs can clearly be seen here.

87. *Whitwell* on Ventnor train about to plunge into the smoke reek of Ventnor tunnel. June 1965

88. Rough weather at Ryde Esplanade in December 1963 greets *Ningwood*

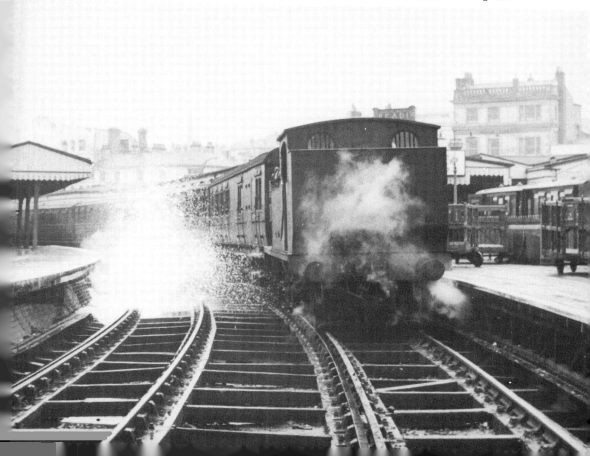

89. Typical Isle of Wight train in the last days *Seaview*, heading out of St John's Road on Cowes train on one of t[
pair of single lines, November 1965

these were to become henceforth the standard engine for the Isle of Wight, and so it was. Still, a five-shilling day trip in 1928 revealed at Newport every sort of engine in the Island, including the Isle of Wight company's *Bonchurch*, the Central's No. 8 and even No. 1, the old contractors' saddle-tank, as well as the Adams O2s and the assorted Brighton 'Terriers' which were then working much of the traffic.

At that time one could travel from Ryde Pier Head to Newport and Cowes in a perfect set of Stroudley four-wheel coaches, or to Ventnor in a Metropolitan rigid eight-wheeler or to Bembridge in a Midland bogie carriage which had proudly served Scotch expresses when those first ran via Settle and Appleby to Carlisle. The best Isle of Wight coaches of those middle nineteen-twenties were ex-London and South Western eight-wheelers, with compensated bogies, dating back to the early eighteen-eighties. Be it remarked that I had just travelled down to Portsmouth in such a carriage, for the mainland survivors were then made up into excursion and trooping sets. Goodness knows what happened to them in the end, but most of the Isle of Wight Metropolitans are on the sea-wall, looking across from St Helens to Bembridge, and remarkably well preserved too, as I write.

Of impressions gained at too-long intervals, be it remarked that by 1928 the carriages, though clean, had a rather moth-eaten aspect. Certainly that went for the trimming. The South Westerns and the Brightons still wore the faded finery in which they had arrived. There was that London Brighton and South Coast art-fabric printed with gory vegetation on a Victorian-ink ground which ultimately mellowed to a colour-scheme of Southwater-brick upon cow-pat, plus dust. The South Western's best third-class uncut-moquette was red-on-black with brown buttons, so respectably stodgy as to pattern, as to be beyond description save that the black ultimately became green, of a sort. But the old Metropolitans—or certainly some of them—were lined with the Highland Railway's falling-leaves plush. Goodness knows how they got it, but it was indestructible stuff and also made good aprons for railway blacksmiths, less vulnerable than leather. I know for certain that it could last in a train for over twenty years. A monograph ought to be written on railways textiles.

Years went by, and another war with the Germans. When I was told in 1948 that all the pride and beauty of old railway tradition still was there in the Isle of Wight, I went back. There were the O2s, in O. V. S. Bulleid's famous malachite green, but with the local variation of yellow lining instead of white. Never had William Adams's now aged tank engines looked more spruce, not even between the old Queen's two Jubilees, when they were new, and old father Adams was still a famous and much-loved figure. Some had their old big domes—which indeed were to be the final form; some had what might have been called a phony-Drummond dome (a Brighton product of the twenties) but *Bembridge* certainly had a real Drummond boiler. She also distinguished herself by running with SOUTHERN, then with a lead-grey blank, and then with BRITISH RAILWAYS on her green tank sides all within a week. In that quaint year of 1948, some of us scarcely realized what was happening to things long familiar. That flimsy-looking lion on a monocycle had not yet come to adorn locomotives and other objects.

Back to carriages: London Chatham and Dover four-wheelers still could be sampled, though I think there were but two. Then there was a London Brighton and South Coast saloon, which had at one end the only working water-closet ever to have been seen on an Isle of Wight train. A notice admonished guards to lock it between Wroxall and Ventnor. At the other end, this singular carriage had a first-class compartment connected by side corridor to an observation compartment with generous windows. I had a very pleasant ride in this last, watching the engine. 'R' said *Godshill*'s driver when he saw me there at Freshwater. 'You do yoursel: well, you do!' At Carisbrooke he got down and again inspected me through the window this time he simply said 'R'. At Newport, after the train had set back into the station, h amiably posed for me; he seemed a big man for little *Godshill*, grinning from her cab like i sardonic Cheshire cat. That was a happy visit. All the Island lines, even the Bembridge branch, were still open.

It was different in 1966. There was one thing to me more deplorable even than the atrophy of the Island's railway system, though a loco-coal train was still working to St John's from Medina Wharf, once Conacher's pride on the Central. It was not so much the black decrepitude of the surviving O2 tank engines—not all had rusty smoke-boxes, and one had her splashe beadings shone up, a nice gesture like a kiss for an old lady. The thing was that the brass nameplates had vanished, not discreetly but to be replaced by horrid little things like tinplate labels, bearing the old names. I was relieved to be reassured later that this had been a pre- cautionary measure because of the likelihood of theft. Though that was a sad enough reflectior of the times we live in, at least it is better than some quick-profit sale to a 'dealer'.

Still over the Pier, half a mile out to sea, on that golden September week-end rolled thosε much-loved little engines, grubby yet proud, and behind them trundled the ancient woodeI coaches which one could remember seeing on Continental Expresses, and on that which thε London Brighton and South Coast so loftily described as ISLE OF WIGHT FAST in a large placard upon the indicator at Victoria. Then on the Sunday, they were terminating at Ryde Esplanade working up and down the tunnel with an engine each end of the train, for there was no running round at the top. It made a miniature suggestion of working up from St David's to Queeı Street at Exeter in the old days.

So began the final passing of the Isle of Wight steam locomotives. They did it decently without fuss.

A visit in mid-November was a chilly and depressing experience in spite of shooting acrosÊ from Southsea to Ryde in a hovercraft in $6\frac{1}{2}$ minutes. The little steam engines were run-dowI and decayed and as a portent of things to come a Hunslet 0–6–0 diesel-mechanical shunteI No. D 2554, once used on Parkeston Quay, Harwich, was lurking at the back of Ryde shed anc the trial coach from the London Underground with its two shepherding adaptor-wagons attached, was in the unused road in St John's Road station, further up which lay 0–4–4 tank No. W18 being cannibalized, three wagons due for preservation and a train of coal trucks.

The hourly service was being maintained with five engines in steam plus a standby and twc three-coach trains which between St John's Road and Esplanade where no run-round waÊ available were operated with an engine at each end. The most notable thing on a footplate run down to Shanklin and back on a perfectly ordinary winter Saturday was the number oi photographers out to record our going; there must have been thirty of them at least.

The day before the day before the Last Day began ill for our wheezy old 'Battle of Britain veteran failed us at Farnborough and a diesel had to be sent for. This dragged our steam engine protesting it almost seemed and the Pullman train, now woefully late, into Southampton. Later, they passed us at the Brockenhurst level crossing, steam still resentfully at the diesel's heels, as we were taxiing to Lymington, the whole programme in jeopardy.

No train down to the pier there to fit the 16.00 boat, so a fierce clandestine walk along thε track was necessary, to catch the ferry to Yarmouth by a whisker.

So began a sentimental journey choosing the route to the Island, first followed on the firs

90. Winter storage at Sandown, 1960. *Brading, Shanklin, Shorwell* and *Alverstone* waiting for the tourists to return

91. The End of the Line 1952, *Bembridge* at Freshwater

92. Early Saturday workings in 1965 and 1966 used double heading to move locomotives from Ryde to where they were needed; here is the 7.40 a.m. train out of Ryde in June 1965

93. This is another Saturday double-headed turn, the first parcels train out of Ryde, the 7.50 a.m. in 196? Nos. 24 and 29 on duty

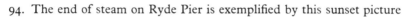

94. The end of steam on Ryde Pier is exemplified by this sunset picture

95. Farewell to the lines to Ventnor and Cowes by the Locomotive Club of Great Britain—and a fleeting reminder of past pride in appearance; *Fishbourne* and *Calbourne* are the engines

96. The essence of the Isle of Wight transport problem, the huge Saturday crowds

visit in 1914. The *Farringford* skittered down the Lymington River past those enjoyable beacons, 'Tar Barrel', 'Bag of Halfpence' and 'Jack in the Basket'. The grey downs of Western Wight loomed along the horizon and Hurst Castle stood up dark grey against a pale grey sky in the failing light, soon illumined by its lighthouse. Further down the Solent the Needles—so clearly seen with the whole diamond island from a BEA 'Comet' two days earlier—were lost in haze but revealed by the intermittent glare of the lighthouse.

A force eight gale blowing up from the west set up a bit of a lop and the ferry took some spray over her bows; it was a cold and bleak winter evening.

Then here was friendly Yarmouth with cosy lights behind red shades, the square in the little town hardly changed in fifty years; true the *Pier Hotel* had become *The George* but the *Bugle* was still there; outside it we children used to watch fascinated the antics of the liberty men, some the better, some the worse for drink, from the Navy of World War I.

The day before the last day was by contrast a beauty and a walk on Tennyson Down before breakfast, with the birds calling in the woods below as if it were spring an exhilarating experience, probably never to be done again. The sun was bright in the sky and all down the Back of the Wight, the spray was boiling off the ledges and headlands of the bays from the overnight gale. 'All sand and cliff and deep in-running cave.' To the west the white cliffs of Swanage showed almost 20 miles away, a portent of rain to come, and over to Hurst Castle and Hampshire it was fine and clear. That morning too yielded some surprises, the first to learn from the researches of Mr Green, the Seely Librarian, into old account books that there had been a railway in the Island in 1833 built by the Nash Estate at Hamstead, east of Yarmouth, for a distance of 2,500 yards, probably to run from their brickworks to a jetty on the Solent. It was clearly hand or horse drawn.

Then Mr Spanner assured us that recent researches had shown that the feud between the IWC and the FYN in 1913 had been so virulent that the two FYN locomotives which had been discharged at St Helens Quay had had to be dragged to Newport by the old steam-hauled equivalent of today's low-loader and lastly that the contractor's engine *Godshill* had been hauled from Merstone to Godshill station to join in the construction of the NG & ST L on the public highway on her own wheels. After that, footplating up to Ryde from Shanklin was almost an anticlimax in spite of the crowds of onlookers already on the ground.

97. While repairs were being done on Ryde Pier in 1963 and 1964 and again after the Pier was closed to passenger trains on 17.9.66 trains had to work from St John's Road to Esplanade with a locomotive at each end

So to the last day. And this broke dark, lowering and wet, fitting weather for tears! The advertised services came and went, several of the engines with an ephemeral cleanliness brought about by dedicated volunteers; the 10.30 from Ryde went out past the silent threatening electric trains parked between St John's and Smallbrook, with a holly wreath and a signboard describing the dread occasion. Then at noon *Calbourne* and *Chale* spruced up a little, like an old aunt putting on the attire of her youth, pulled forward to the side road, to back onto the up five-coach 12.07 from St John's Road. So up to Esplanade where a huge crowd presented itself, no less than 510 persons on the special train from London plus local adherents. So, soon after 12.15 we were away, *Chale* leading, and after a stop at St John's to shed our banker we fled south, an express to Shanklin, no less, passing the crowded stations at Brading and Sandown and the innumerable photographers en route on signal posts, bridges, banks and in the sodden fields. As we got to Shanklin a sad wet cloud came over the Down but soon after it turned to duck-egg-blue sky and some sun to reward the faithful. That was the *Special*— and it was so labelled—but meanwhile the regular hourly services were continuing.

Fittingly enough, Pattern I, the hardest roster of all, starting in the small hours of the morning with mail and parcels and ending with the last train was reserved for No. W14 *Fishbourne* the oldest engine in the Island and believed to be the oldest in all Britain in regular service which was built in 1889. So at 22.12 the last passenger train left Shanklin with a huge crowd of well-wishers, sentimental observers and those just plain curious to perform the last steam-hauled service in the Isle of Wight.

This was almost a moment of tears, certainly of ghostly memories—of handsome Isle of Wight crimson engines with their wild shrieking whistles, of Isle of Wight Central hooters, perpetuated in the O2s of today, braying as the trains ran into the small tunnels at the head of their teak coaches, the three-axle beat of the little FYN engines snaking down to the Calbourne viaduct, the charming Brading Harbour branch, the glorious downland scenery, the primroses in the woods and the boat trains rumbling up the pier to meet the paddle-steamers. Dear God 'to say goodbye, it is to die a little'.

'Fret not to roam the desert now, with all thy winged speed:
I may not mount on thee again! thou'rt sold my Arab steed'.

POSTSCRIPT 1986

In the intervening nineteen years since the first edition of this book was published, there have been a number of important changes to record, events far happier than one would have dared hope in those anti-railway days of the mid 1960s.

Passenger trains recommenced running between Ryde Pier Head and Shanklin on 20 March 1967. Services provided have naturally varied over the years, but have always been more frequent than the steam services they replaced. Although it was never officially made public, the old London Transport Tube stock was given a maximum life of ten years, and it was confidently predicted the line would be closed by 1975. Passenger figures, however, remained buoyant, and for some years have been increasing due to the general decline in local bus services coupled with a competitive fare structure. In the interests of economy, track rationalisation has taken place wherever possible, and careful stock working has enabled several cars to be scrapped. The double line has been retained from Ryde to Smallbrook where entry onto the single line section is controlled remotely from St John's Road signal box. The final two miles from Sandown to Shanklin is now worked under the 'one train operation' arrangement from Sandown. The two original Isle of Wight Railway signal boxes still survive at Brading and Sandown, while Brading Station has the distinction of being the last on the whole of British Rail to be lit by gas. At Ryde, the Pier, while retaining the appearance of double track, is in reality two single lines, a crossover at Esplanade remotely controlled from St John's Road enabling a train to shut in on the former down line to form a shuttle service up and down the pier. This proved an effective replacement for the tramway service which was life expired and withdrawn in 1969, and made possible the closure of Pier Head signal box. At the time of writing the future looks brighter than it has done for many years past despite the very great age of the rolling stock. Car No. S43 became something of a *cause célèbre* on achieving its Diamond Jubilee on 28 January 1984, and Ryde Works for the first time in its 120 year history was thrown open to the public for the day. All the vehicles are now well past their half century, but there are at present no positive plans for replacement. The Hunslet diesel shunter, latterly numbered 97803 was replaced by a 204hp Drewry, No. 03 079, one of British Rail's standard classes, in April 1984.

As the British Rail steam era in the Isle of Wight drew to a close, another one was about to begin! An appeal for funds, mainly on the last day of steam, by the Wight Locomotive Society, resulted in the purchase of one of the final O2s, No. 24 *Calbourne*, and five passenger coaches for preservation. Following the abandonment of the Vectrail Society's proposals, some wagons and the Midland Railway crane were also obtained. This collection was stored initially at Newport, *Calbourne* having to be brought from Ryde by road, and the bold notion was conceived of buying the section of line from Haven Street to Wootton and setting up a working museum. On 24 January 1971, *Calbourne* hauled the preserved vehicles from Newport to Haven Street in four trains, and the demolition contractors moved in on the remainder of the Ryde to Cowes line the following day. Thus was born the Isle of Wight Steam Railway, which has gone from strength to strength and thoroughly consolidated its position in the following fourteen years up to the present time. A considerable number of additional locomotives and vehicles have been obtained from various sources. No account of the present day scene at Haven Street could fail to mention the return to the Isle of Wight of two of the Stroudley 'Terriers', No. 8 *Freshwater* (formerly FYNR No. 2) and No. 11 *Newport*, the Paris Gold Medallist of 1878, and later No. 11 in the Isle of Wight Central fleet.

98. W22 *Brading* on a Cowes train near Smallbrook Junction in 1964. The line was being worked as two single lines.

9. Surely a remarkable photograph—repair work inside Ryde tunnel with a Ventnor train passing by, 1966.

Mechanical restoration of *Newport* is well under way, and *Freshwater* has put in much useful work since being restored to working order in 1981. The Isle of Wight Steam Railway has also amassed a collection of historic carriage bodies which are still sound after many years' use as beach huts, farmyard stores and the like. The long term aim is to recreate a Victorian train using suitable replacement underframes, and of these an old North London Railway vehicle of 1864 vintage, for many years No. 46 on the Isle of Wight Railway, should be in traffic in 1986. These ambitious projects have been made possible by building a well-equipped works at Haven Street, and the high standard of workmanship and the ability to make something out of nothing preserves the spirit of the Isle of Wight Central in a unique and very personal way. The Haven Street complex is completed by a tastefully designed museum with an ever growing number of exhibits.

Developments have continued apace with regard to the shipping services, and none of the car ferries mentioned in the first edition now remains in service. Six vessels, some interchangeable, now maintain the Portsmouth to Fishbourne and Lymington to Yarmouth routes, the latest two *St Helen* and *St Catherine* introduced on the Fishbourne service in 1983, being the largest vessels ever employed on cross-Solent duties. Greatly enlarged terminals in keeping with the increased volume of traffic have been brought into use at Portsmouth, Fishbourne and Lymington. A decline in the number of classic passengers, coupled with intensive diagramming, has enabled the Portsmouth to Ryde passenger route to be reduced to two vessels only. At the time of writing *Brading* and *Southsea* continue to maintain the service for which they were built in 1948 but it is anticipated they will shortly be replaced with two or three lightweight catamarans. Once again there is a story of preservation; *Ryde*, the final paddle steamer withdrawn in 1969, was towed to Binfield on the River Medina, where she survives as the clubhouse of a yacht marina.

95

(*left*) 100. The shape of the future; diesel-mechanical locomotive No. D2554 on Ryde Pier, October 1966

(*below*) 101. More portents; London Transport Tube coach made up with adaptor wagon to test clearances, September 1966

(*opposite top*) 102. A typical view to remind us that it was always a small railway with a very narrow right of way. *Ventnor* on Apse Bank 1965

(*opposite below*) 103. The end of the steam era. Ryde train leaving Shanklin with *Seaview*, December 30, 1966. The conductor rails for the new electric service are clearly visible

104. The last day of steam. Locomotive Club of Great Britain special express at the summit of Brading Bank, December 31, 1966. One of the authors is on the footplate of *Chale*, the pilot engine. The train engine is *Calbourne*

104a. The last steam passenger train at Shanklin, 22.12, December 31, 1966, locomotive No. W14 *Fishbourne*

ppendix I

NOTES ON ROLLING STOCK AND LIVERIES IN THE ISLAND

le 1 shows some particulars of all the locomotives owned by the Island railways from 1861 to 1923
n the Southern Railway took over, sixteen owned by the Isle of Wight Central, eight by the Isle of
ht and two by the Freshwater, Yarmouth & Newport.
he oldest engines of the IWCR were the two original 2–2–2 well tanks of the Cowes & Newport.
 they came ashore and where is a mystery. When built they had no cabs and tall copper-capped
neys, wooden brake blocks and sandboxes on the footplate; they ended life with cabs, stove pipe
neys and sandboxes on the boiler. Originally painted light blue they later changed to the dark
of the mid years of the Central before the departure of the spacious Mr Conacher, the General
ager, to the Cambrian in 1910. The two 1876 Beyer Peacock 2–4–0 tanks of the Ryde & Newport
 originally green with brass numbers on the sides of the chimneys, wooden brake blocks and buffer
ns and injectors on top of the tanks; they later were painted red and finally black. No. 5 ended her
in Southern 'sage-green'. Little No. 3 built in 1870 was olive-green lined out with white when built.
he other IWCR engines started life painted first red and then black. Some of the engines at some
es carried the title of the railway on a garter with the number within and at others the full name
ne railway painted on the tank sides. When black livery, lined out in red and white became the
dard, the title of the line was restricted to 'IWC'.
he Isle of Wight Railway engines were always red but, we think. rather a dark brick red in their
 days ending with a good dark Midland-red paint by the end of World War I, with a thin yellow
and black edging to tanks and bunkers.
n the FY & N the Manning Wardle tank No. 1 spent its life until repainted by the Southern, with
d-green livery and lettered first 'FY & N Rly' and later FYN. The 'Terrier' No. 2 ran in LSWR colours
d a Drummond boiler—from the date of purchase until 1919 when it emerged in bright light
n, almost like the 1947 LNER green, lined out with black and white with red side rods, lettered
'. While the IWC 'Terriers' were given enlarged coal bunkers, No. 2 did not acquire one until the
thern took over.
he second table (Table 2) shows all the locomotives which served in the Island under the Southern
British Railways régimes.
he original Southern locomotive livery was always, for some reason, described as 'sage-green'
:h, for anyone acquainted with a sage bush, it certainly was not. In fact the colour was a true olive-
n, exactly the colour of a good green olive. Next, the engines were repainted in what might be
:ribed as a 'dark apple-green', far bluer than the first shade, in fact a good solid mid-green; this
1ge was made in 1925. Later, when O. V. S. Bulleid became Chief Mechanical Engineer, the SR
ur was changed again to malachite green, as bright a mid-green as there is which was intended to
ined out in yellow and black. Though malachite green was adopted by the SR in 1940, by then the
was on and the bright lights were dimmed, and black with a variety of lettering prevailed. However,
re the war ended some painting in unlined malachite green was possible so that by the war's end
e were several variants of the Southern livery to be seen. Thus in 1947 it was possible to observe
ne Island the old green colour, unlined, malachite green, unlined, black with yellow lettering, shaded
reen, and then finally the fully lined-out malachite green which was introduced before the end of
5 on several of the O2 tanks and very smart it looked with the scarlet buffer beams and backgrounds
ne brass nameplates, far far removed from the drab austerity continuing on the mainland. The little
:rier' W13 looked especially good with her copper-topped chimney.
ery soon after Nationalization on January 1, 1948, with indecent haste it seemed to some, the
thern name was erased from locomotives' flanks and 'British Railways' substituted. However, the
d-out malachite green remained and continued especially to adorn W13 who with her brasswork
ed and her paint glistening was conspicuous on the Ventnor West branch. Then the British Railways
dard livery of black lined out with grey, cream and red began to come in in 1949 and at the same
it the emaciated lion balancing on a bicycle wheel began to appear on tank sides, to be replaced in

1957 by the half lion emerging from the crown holding a crumpet. The last repainting in the Island that of No. W24 in 1966 left her with the badge but in unlined black.

At least British Railways did nothing to get rid of the Island locomotives' nameplates, nothing that is until 1965 when they had to be removed to safeguard them from thieves, values having risen giddily The nameplates had been a feature in IWR days and their reintroduction by the Southern on all loco motives in 1928 was a popular move; they were well made in cast brass with a red ground for the lettering.

There was always some confusion among the O2 tank engines because some had Drummond boiler with the brass-cased safety valves striking out of the dome and others the Adams boiler with a big plain dome and Ramsbottom safety valves over the firebox. At one point Nos. W17–W26 had the Adam boiler and Nos W27–W32 the Drummond. On reboilering, like did not always replace like though toward the end of affairs in the Island the Adams boiler became more and more the standard, though No. 2 *Brading*, one of the three scheduled to be kept on into 1967, retained a Drummond boiler until the end and No. 31 *Chale* was given one as late as 1962 or 1963.

Contractors' and other locomotives

Knowledge of what we might call visiting locomotives is confused and imprecise. While the first sod of the Cowes and Newport Railway was cut in 1859 its first locomotives were built in 1861 so it can be inferred that the early construction work was carried out by the aid of horsepower and that the two tank engines then set to work until the opening of the line on June 16, 1862.

The Ryde & Newport Railway was built we believe with the aid of a 0–4–0 outside cylinder saddle tank called *Bee* built by Hughes & Co. One unconfirmed report has it that this engine was later the first No. 6 in the Joint Committee's books—but then so was the *Newport* of the IW(NJ)R. The *Bee* was last reported to us as doing occasional duty at Medina Wharf, Cowes, as a spare for No. 3 of the Cowe & Newport and eventually sold and shipped away by barge in 1884 or thereabouts.

The Isle of Wight (Newport Junction) line was built with the aid of a Beattie 2–2–2 well tank engine hired from the London & South Western Railway which, Michael Robbins tells us, cost them £2 a day and the crew's wages; this locomotive, No. 36 *Comet*, came over in 1872 but we don't know when it retired although the line engine, the 2–2–2 well tank from the Furness (*Queen Mab* later *Newport*) arrived in 1875. It is likely too that the NJR hired locomotive-time from the IWR both for construction and running.

Information has been scanty as to what contractors' locomotives were used on the construction of the Isle of Wight Railway from Ryde to Ventnor but an article has just reached us which gives the name of an 0–4–2 contractors' locomotive called *Grafton* built by Hawthorn's of Leith which was sold out of the Island in 1866 to Messrs Furniss who are believed to have used it on the Hayling Island construction It changed hands again and ended up with the name of *Brighton*, at, of all places, Brunner, Mond' chemical works at Northwich—now part of ICI.

The contractors for the St Helens and Bembridge branch, the ownership of which was not taken over by the IWR until 1898, used two engines in building the line, the *St Helens* and the *Bembridge* (formerly said to have been called *Stanley*). The latter worked the branch for years after it was built in 1882 and was later taken into the IWR stock and finally went away to World War I. The *St Helens* was a 2–4–0 saddle tank with a haystack firebox, cast-iron wheels and round coupling and connecting rods. The IWR Works Repair Books show her as undergoing repairs in 1882 and 1884 so she probably worked the branch too for a time. She was then reported as working on the construction of the Newport, Godshill & St Lawrence line but was by then worn out. She lay for some while in Whitwell siding and was re ported as broken up there in about 1897. Also used on this branch was a Kerr Stuart[1] 0–6–0 saddle tank called *Godshill* which was taken out of the Island by Westwoods the contractors when the work was finished, ending up on the GCR Marylebone–St John's Wood construction. They also employed a special engine on the St Lawrence tunnel construction, a diminutive 0–4–0 tank, with a cut-down chimney called *Weaste* built by Hudswell Clarke which as its name suggests was once engaged on the building of the Manchester Ship Canal; it left at the same time as *Godshill*.

The Freshwater line was built with the aid of a 0–6–0 side tank called *Freshwater* built by Robt Stephenson & Co. in 1887 and later sold to the Weston Clevedon and Portishead Railway. She finished life with the Renishaw Iron Company in Derbyshire and survived to 1936. The earlier work on the

[1] One authority says she was built by the Worcester Engine Co. and rebuilt by Kerr Stuart.

105. *The development of No. 11* Upper: As she was on the LB & SCR after winning the Gold Medal in Paris in 1878

106. Centre: In IWCR colours 1919

107. Lower: In her last state with LSWR chimney, 1933

108. *The development of* Wroxall. Upper: As she was in 1913 with copper-capped chimney.

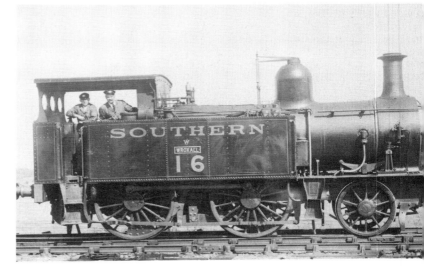

109. Centre: In 1924 style in Southern Green with IWR chimney.

110. Lower: In her last state with IWCR cab and LSWR chimney, 1932

shwater line is said to have used one of the old Ryde Pier steam tram engines. The *Freshwater* was subject of a dispute between the contractors building the line and the FY & NR so that while it was g repaired in Ryde shops it was chained to the rails and kept under guard until satisfaction was ined, though another version of the story says that it was the IWR who chained it down and refused elease it until the repairs had been paid for.

ching and Wagon Stock

'he IWCR had a great variety of coaches, mostly four-wheelers, which had been bought from such nland railways as the LNWR, MR, GER, LB & SCR & NLR. The company did, however, possess four ie coaches which had an interesting history.

'he first bogie coaches to run in the Island were two which were built for the company by the caster Carriage & Wagon Company in 1889. They were short, as bogie coaches go, being only 40 over buffers, one was a composite 1st and 2nd, the other a composite brake and were used up to 3 prior to the fracas with the FYNR in that year, for the through services between Ryde & Freshwater. :ing World War I the 2nd Class compartments were relabelled 3rd.

1 1906 when railcars were fashionable one was purchased from Hawthorn Leslie, which consisted small 0-4-0 steam side tank engine (IWCR No. 1) and an open coach with a rear driving and luggage apartment, the engine acting as the second coach bogie. In 1907 in order to operate a second railcar, company bought a twelve-wheeled composite compartment coach from the Midland Railway, ;eet long, built in 1875, which had been used on the St Pancras, Carlisle & Edinburgh Expresses. lriving and luggage compartment was put in at one end and the Medina Wharf shunting engine 3 (0-4-2 saddle tank) was used to pull or push it as a railcar. No. 3's boiler, cab and bunker were ;red over with iron sheeting to give the engine a more massive appearance.

)uring the next few years, both these units operated but neither railcar was really successful and in 1 both locomotives were relegated to shunting work and were finally sold in 1918 for construction k in the Furness Withy Dock extension at Middlesbrough. The open coach from the original railcar fitted with a second bogie and with the ex-MR 12-wheeler, also a brake composite, ran with the r-wheelers in service trains.

after World War I the twelve-wheeler was rebogied as an eight-wheeler, with two bogies bought from :by and the clerestory on the coach roof was cut down for extra clearance under tunnels and bridges. ;he IWC also had a four-wheeled saloon which it is stated had twenty-two seats, and was available for or 2nd class passengers. This coach lasted until 1926 when the SR replaced it by an ex-LBSC four-:eled vehicle for inspection purposes. The coaching stock was finished in varnished teak or mahogany n gilt lettering. The wagons, many of which were constructed at Newport, were a varied collection it is known that one of the brake vans came from the MR. The wagons were mostly painted in grey, some were black, the lettering being in white.

;he IWR also purchased its coaches from the mainland, the majority being four-wheelers from the rth London Railway. Some were also purchased which had been intended for a South American lway.

;he most interesting vehicles were eighteen coaches from the Metropolitan Railway—eight-wheelers h fixed axles—which were only 39' 6" long and weighed 17 tons. These were composites and thirds, latter having eight compartments and seats for eighty passengers. These lasted up to 1929 and many he bodies can be seen to this day in use as bathing huts at St Helens opposite Bembridge Harbour uth. When the horse trams were no longer required on Ryde Pier in 1886, two of them were bought the IWR for use on the Brading–Bembridge branch. These made very popular saloons after strengthen- and fitting with a third pair of wheels. They later were converted to six-wheeled brake and luggage .s. All coaches were finished in varnished teak, the number of the vehicle being painted in gilt inside IWR garter below the waist line. The assorted wagon stock was painted in red oxide with white ering. The majority were built in Ryde works.

;he FYNR provided its own rolling stock from 1913. All the coaches were four-wheeled and made up trains of six coaches: one was made up of LSWR stock, the other with old Manchester, Sheffield & colnshire (later Great Central Railway) vehicles which were no longer required on the Manchester th Junction & Altrincham line, where they had been working, as new bogie stock was being built this mainland service. All the FYN coaches were varnished teak. The limited wagon stock had also been chased from the mainland and were painted grey with white lettering. It is interesting to note that ie of the cattle wagons had corrugated iron roofs.

Rails in the Isle of Wight

TABLE I
LOCOMOTIVES OF THE ISLE OF WIGHT RAILWAYS
[All tank engines]

Number	Name	Type	Builder	Date built	Date bought	Disposal
1. ISLE OF WIGHT CENTRAL						
1	Pioneer	2–2–2	Slaughter Gruning (453)	1861		Scrapped 1904
1		0–4–0	Hawthorn Leslie (2669)	1906		Sold 1918
1	Precursor	2–2–2	Slaughter Gruning (454)	1861		Scrapped 1904
2		0–4–4	Marquess of Londonderry's Railway—Seaham	1895	1909	Sold 1917
3		0–4–2	Black Hawthorn (116)	1870		Sold 1918
4	Cowes	2–4–0	Beyer Peacock (1583)	1876		To SR 1923
5	Osborne	2–4–0	Beyer Peacock (1584)	1876		To SR 1923
6	Newport	2–2–2	Hawthorn (1128)	1861	1875	Duplicate list 189 Scrapped 1895
6		4–4–0	Black Hawthorn (999)	1890		To SR 1923
7		4–4–0	Slaughter Gruning (443)	1861	1880	Scrapped 1906
7		2–4–0	Beyer Peacock (2231)	1882	1906	To SR 1923
8		2–4–0	Beyer Peacock (3942)	1898		To SR 1923
9		0–6–0	Brighton	1872	1899	To SR 1923
10		0–6–0	Brighton	1874	1900	To SR 1923
11		0–6–0	Brighton	1878	1902	To SR 1923
12		0–6–0	Brighton	1880	1903	To SR 1923
2. ISLE OF WIGHT RAILWAY						
	Ryde	2–4–0	Beyer Peacock (400)	1864		To SR 1923
	Sandown	2–4–0	Beyer Peacock (401)	1864		To SR 1923
	Shanklin	2–4–0	Beyer Peacock (402)	1864		To SR 1923
	Ventnor	2–4–0	Beyer Peacock (848)	1868		To SR 1923
	Wroxall	2–4–0	Beyer Peacock (1141)	1872		To SR 1923
	Brading	2–4–0	Beyer Peacock (1638)	1876		To SR 1923
	Bonchurch	2–4–0	Beyer Peacock (2376)	1883		To SR 1923
	Bembridge	0–6–0	Manning Wardle (517)	1875	1882	To war service 1917
3. FRESHWATER, YARMOUTH AND NEWPORT						
1		0–6–0	Manning Wardle (1555)	1902	1913	To SR 1923
2		0–6–0	Brighton	1876	1913	To SR 1923

Also four-wheeled Drewry railcar 20 h.p.—4 cylinders   90 mm. × 130 mm.   2 ft diameter wheels.

Previous owner	Driving Wheels	Cylinders	Weight	Remarks
wes and Newport	5 ft	13½ in × 16 in	19·2 tons	
	3 ft 6 in	9 in × 14 in	15·5 tons	To Holloway Bros. for Middlesbrough Docks
wes and Newport	5 ft	13½ in × 16 in	19·2 tons	
ndonderry Rly (21) R (1712)	5 ft 4½ in	17 in × 24 in	45·3 tons	To Armstrong Whitworth at Elswick
wes and Newport	3 ft 3 in	10 in × 17 in	15·5 tons	To Holloway Bros. as above
de and Newport	5 ft	14 in × 20 in	26·4 tons	
de and Newport	5 ft	14 in × 20 in	26·4 tons	
aitehaven and Furness, urness (46) 7. (Newport Junction)	5 ft 6 in	14 in × 20 in	?	
	5 ft 3 in	16 in × 22 in	40 tons	
R (35 and 106) oint Committee	5 ft 3 in	15½ in × 22 in	34·5 tons	
WJR (No. 6)	5 ft 6 in	16¼ in × 24 in	35·2 tons	
	5 ft 1 in	14 in × 20 in	30·8 tons	
CR (75) *Blackwall*	4 ft	14 in × 20 in	24·3 tons	
CR (69) *Peckham*	4 ft	14 in × 20 in	24·3 tons	
CR (40) *Brighton*	4 ft	14 in × 20 in	24·3 tons	Gold medallist Paris 1878
CR (84) *Crowborough*	4 ft	14 in × 20 in	24·3 tons	
	5 ft	15 in × 20 in	30·4 tons	
	5 ft	15 in × 20 in	30·4 tons	
	5 ft	15 in × 20 in	30·4 tons	
	5 ft	15 in × 20 in	30·4 tons	
	5 ft ½ in	15 in × 20 in	31·7 tons	
	5 ft ½ in	16 in × 24 in	34·4 tons	
	5 ft ½ in	17 in × 24 in	35·7 tons	
rbour branch contractor	3 ft	13 in × 18 in		To War Dept 1917
G. Pauling (56) *Northolt*	3 ft 6 in	14 in × 20 in	27 tons	Contractor's loco on High Wycombe line
VR (734): LBSCR (46) *Newington*	4 ft	13 in × 20 in	24·3 tons	Ex LSWR Lyme Regis branch

TABLE 2

LOCOMOTIVES OF THE SOUTHERN AND BRITISH RAILWAYS
[All tank engines]

Number	Name	Type	Previous owner (and number)	Date built	Date to Island	Disposal
A. ISLAND LOCOMOTIVES						
1	*Medina*	0–6–0	FYN (1)	1902	1913	Scrapped 1932
2 later 8	*Freshwater*	0–6–0	FYN (2)	1876	1913	To mainland 1949
4		2–4–0	IWC (4)	1876	1876	Scrapped 1925
5		2–4–0	IWC (5)	1876	1876	Scrapped 1926
6		4–4–0	IWC (6)	1890	1890	Scrapped 1926
7		2–4–0	IWC (7)	1882	1908	Scrapped 1926
8		2–4–0	IWC (8)	1898	1898	Scrapped 1929
9		0–6–0	IWC (9)	1872	1899	Scrapped 1927
10	*Cowes*	0–6–0	IWC (10)	1874	1900	To mainland 1936
11	*Newport*	0–6–0	IWC (11)	1878	1902	To mainland 1947
12	*Ventnor*	0–6–0	IWC (12)	1880	1903	To mainland 1936
13	*Ryde*	2–4–0	IWR	1864	1864	Withdrawn 1932 (scrapped 1940)
	Sandown	2–4–0	IWR	1864	1864	Scrapped 1923
14	*Shanklin*	2–4–0	IWR	1864	1864	Scrapped 1927
15	*Ventnor*	2–4–0	IWR	1868	1868	Scrapped 1925
16	*Wroxall*	2–4–0	IWR	1872	1872	Scrapped 1933
17	*Brading*	2–4–0	IWR	1876	1876	Scrapped 1926
18	*Bonchurch*	2–4–0	IWR	1883	1883	Scrapped 1928

B. SOUTHERN IMPORTS

(iii) *Class A1x* [Driving wheels 4 ft; cylinders 12, 13 or 14 in × 20 in; weight 27 tons]

Number	Name	Type	Previous owner (and number)	Date built	Date to Island	Disposal
3 later 13	*Carisbrooke*	0–6–0	LBSC (77) *Wonersh*	1880	1927	To mainland 1949
4 later 14	*Bembridge*	0–6–0	LBSC (78) *Knowle*	1880	1929	To mainland 1936
9	*Fishbourne*	0–6–0	LBSC (50) *Whitechapel*	1876	1930	To mainland 1936

(ii) *Class E1* [Driving wheels 4 ft 6 in; cylinders 17 in × 24 in; weight 44·5 tons]

Number	Name	Type	Previous owner (and number)	Date built	Date to Island	Disposal
1	*Medina*	0–6–0	LBSC (136) *Brindisi*	1878	1932	Scrapped 1957
2	*Yarmouth*	0–6–0	LBSC (152) *Hungary*	1880	1932	Scrapped 1956
3	*Ryde*	0–6–0	LBSC (154) *Madrid*	1881	1932	Scrapped 1959
4	*Wroxall*	0–6–0	LBSC (131) *Gournay*	1878	1933	Scrapped 1961

mber	Name	Type	Previous owner (and number)	Date built	Date to Island	Disposal
) *Class O2* [Driving wheels 4 ft 10 in; cylinders $17\frac{1}{2}$ in $\times$ 24 in; weight 44·6 to 48·9 tons]						
4	*Fishbourne*	0–4–4	LSWR (178)	1889	1936	
5	*Cowes*	0–4–4	LSWR (195)	1890	1936	Scrapped 1956
6	*Ventnor*	0–4–4	LSWR (217)	1892	1936	
7	*Seaview*	0–4–4	LSWR (208)	1891	1930	
8	*Ningwood*	0–4–4	LSWR (220)	1892	1930	Withdrawn 1966
9	*Osborne*	0–4–4	LSWR (206)	1891	1923	Scrapped 1956
o	*Shanklin*	0–4–4	LSWR (211)	1892	1923	
I	*Sandown*	0–4–4	LSWR (205)	1891	1924	Scrapped 1966
2	*Brading*	0–4–4	LSWR (215)	1892	1924	
3	*Totland*	0–4–4	LSWR (188)	1890	1925	Scrapped 1955
4	*Calbourne*	0–4–4	LSWR (209)	1891	1925	
5	*Godshill*	0–4–4	LSWR (190)	1890	1925	Scrapped 1963
6	*Whitwell*	0–4–4	LSWR (210)	1891	1925	Scrapped 1966
7	*Merstone*	0–4–4	LSWR (184)	1890	1926	
8	*Ashey*	0–4–4	LSWR (186)	1890	1926	
9	*Alverstone*	0–4–4	LSWR (202)	1891	1926	Scrapped 1966
o	*Shorwell*	0–4–4	LSWR (219)	1892	1926	Scrapped 1965
I	*Chale*	0–4–4	LSWR (180)	1890	1927	
2	*Bonchurch*	0–4–4	LSWR (226)	1892	1928	Scrapped 1965
3	*Bembridge*	0–4–4	LSWR (218)	1892	1936	
4	*Newport*	0–4–4	LSWR (201)	1891	1947	Scrapped 1955
5	*Freshwater*	0–4–4	LSWR (181)	1890	1949	Withdrawn 1966
6	*Carisbrooke*	0–4–4	LSWR (198)	1891	1949	Scrapped 1965
Class E4 [Driving wheels 5 ft; cylinders $17\frac{1}{2}$ in $\times$ 26 in; weight 51 tons]						
o		0–6–2	LBSC (510) *Twineham*	1900	1947	To mainland 1948
Diesel — Mechanical [204 h.p.; wheels 3 ft 4 in; weight 30 tons]						
554		0–6–0	BR (E)	1955	1966	Hunslet built

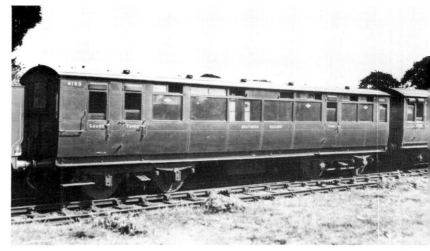

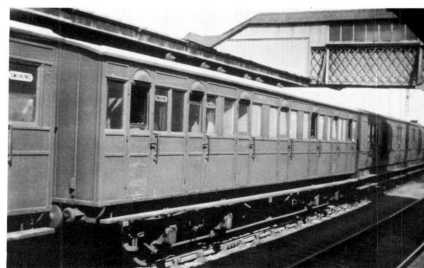

111. Ex-Railmotor coach from IWCR days, at Freshwater 1937

112. Ex-Metropolitan eight-wheeled non-bogie coach from IWR at Brading 1929

113. Slinging ex-LBSC Invalid bogie saloon ashore, Medina Wharf 1932

114. Ex-Midland twelve-wheeled coach which was built in 1875, rebuilt with eight-wheel bogies with clerestory removed: at Ryde St John's Road 1932

115. *Special wagon stock in the 1930s.* Upper: Weed-killing tank cars.

116. Centre: Boiler truck with geared shunter *Midget*.

117. Lower: Special brake van with sanding gear

In Southern Railway days, some interesting rolling stock was sent over at various times. There were the ex-LBSC Stroudley and Billinton four-wheelers made up into set trains, also many ex-LCDR four-wheelers (which were originally six-wheelers) made up into close coupled sets. Nine ex-LSWR low-roofed bogie vehicles were transferred to the Island for working between Cowes and Ryde and Cowes and Sandown; they all had early Pullman type bogies and had been built by the Birmingham Carriage & Wagon Company between 1881 and 1885. Four ex-SE & CR bogie open coaches were sent over in the early SR days fitted up for pull & push working but were not satisfactory and were returned in 1927. They had been originally the coach portion of the steam railcars which had latterly run as two articulated units on the SE section but were altered to separate bogie coaches before coming to the Island. The passenger coaches sent over from 1931 by the SR were eight-wheeled bogie vehicles first of the ex-LCDR type and were then followed by similar ex-LB & SCR ones. The ex-LB & SCR four-wheeled inspection saloon was withdrawn in 1934 and replaced by the old LBSC bogie invalid saloon. This vehicle was altered before coming over as a composite brake coach, which could be used in traffic as well as for inspections.

From 1923–36 the coaches were painted in SR standard deep mid-green lined out with chrome yellow and black, gilt lettering and black shading. Later the colour was changed to malachite green unlined, with lettering of gold, also shaded in black.

The SR gradually replaced the majority of the old Island wagons. The standard coal wagon was the 10 ton ex-LBSC type, many of which were built new on the mainland to the old LBSC specification. The covered vans, cattle trucks and bolster wagons were also of LBSC origin. The brake vans were ex-LSWR road van brakes. The goods stock was painted in the SR dark umber colour with white letters. Ballast wagons, many of SECR origin were painted in SR red oxide with white letters.

From 1948 when Nationalization took place, replacement passenger coaches were SECR bogies converted at Lancing works from the old 'Trio' sets. The 'birdcage' look-outs above the guards' compartments were removed and the lavatories in the composite coaches were converted into ordinary compartment seating. Under British Railways the coach colour up to 1954 was Crimson Lake (a crushed raspberry shade) with a limited lining of yellow and black and 'Gill Sans' style yellow lettering. After this date the standard BR (Southern Region) mid-green was applied unlined with the same lettering.

One interesting item is worth mentioning that when the two old IWR tar tanks were withdrawn in 1947, BR replaced them on the Island by sending over two six-wheeled tenders from Adams A12 class 0–4–2 locomotives fitted up for tar traffic but these were sent back in 1950 when this traffic ceased.

Under BR the wagon stock was painted a light grey with white lettering with service wagons black.

Appendix II

SIGNALLING

Before 1923 mainland-type semaphore signals were used on the Island Railways, wooden arms with wooden posts. After this date, when the SR took over, any renewals of posts and arms which were required were replaced by metal semaphores and lattice-type posts, still with lower quadrant operation. After the war in the 1950s upper quadrant signals were introduced.

The single line sections were worked by various systems and can be briefly described as follows:

The line between Ryde St John's Road and Ventnor was originally worked under the staff and ticket system, but was converted to Webb & Thompson electric staff in IWR days, and this large electric staff working has continued except on the two subsequent double line sections between Ryde St John's Road and Smallbrook Junction and Brading and Sandown referred to later.

Appendix II

The Bembridge branch was worked under the one engine in steam arrangement, but signals were also provided —for what reason it is not clear. At St Helens a signal box was also provided and the up and down home signals were duly interlocked. On the weighbridge house at St Helens Quay a fan shaped signal was used to regulate the movement of the engine when weighing wagons. Presented square on it meant STOP, edge on ALL RIGHT, and waggled to and fro SET BACK. In SR days the signals were all removed, except the Brading Quay distants. Marker lights were installed at St Helens and Bembridge.

Before the amalgamation the only double line was on the joint LSW and LB & SCR section from Ryde Pier Head through Ryde Esplanade to Ryde St John's Road. Here the standard three position block instruments were used. It is interesting to note that when this line was first opened in 1880, the LB & SCR type signals installed had BLACK stripes instead of WHITE painted on the red side of the arms facing the traffic. Early in the SR days an extension of this double line was made to Smallbrook Junction, a scissors crossing being installed at the end of the two parallel single lines (Ryde St John's Road to Brading and Ryde St John's Road to Ashey on the Newport line). A small signal box was provided at Smallbrook which was opened from May to September and the standard three position block instruments used. In the winter a reversion to two single lines from St John's Road applied. Also in early SR days the line was doubled from Brading to Sandown and this portion was worked by the same type of mainland instruments.

Between Ryde St John's Road and Ashey a Tyer's No. 7a tablet instrument was used but this was replaced by a miniature electric staff instrument, when the SR made the passing place between Ryde and Newport at Haven Street. Between Ashey and Newport South an early form of Tyers tablet was used, but this was replaced by a No. 6 electric tablet between Haven Street and Newport South by the SR.

Between Newport South and Shide, No. 4 tablet instruments were used, with a No. 6 between Shide and Merstone. The SR used the No. 4 instruments right through from Newport South to Merstone. From Merstone to Sandown, staff and ticket with Preece's single wire instrument were used, with an intermediate block post (with no passing place) at Newchurch and this arrangement still applied under the SR.

From Merstone to Ventnor Town was also worked by Preece's staff and ticket system with a passing place and block post at Whitwell, but in SR days the loop was removed and the whole section from Merstone to Ventnor Town (now Ventnor West) was worked as a one engine in steam branch.

The technical double line and loop between the north and south signal boxes at Newport were also worked by Preece's one wire position instruments. At Newport South the home signals from both Ryde and Sandown were originally fixed at 'Danger' and all trains were admitted to the platform by 'calling-on' arms placed beneath the homes. These two lines passed over a drawbridge before reaching Newport; this was divided for each track and was operated separately by a hand winch on a cam gear. These bridges were interlocked with the signals and were required to allow sailing barges to proceed up the Medina River to the various wharfs in Newport. This system still worked in SR days.

The section between Cowes & Newport was worked by Tyer's No. 7a tablet instruments, with an intermediate instrument at Medina Wharf Junction to enable a train to be put away there; this arrangement still applied under SR management.

At Medina Wharf weighbridge a semaphore signal was also installed and was misused to give the following indications: Horizontal (Red) STOP, 45° (Green) ALL RIGHT, and 90° when the spectacle was away from the lamp altogether and a white light showing SET BACK. This was done away with when the new deep-water quay was brought into use.

The FYN line was worked under the staff and ticket system throughout, with Sykes simple one wire instruments. Passing loops were provided at Carisbrooke, Ningwood and Yarmouth, Calbourne being a block post but not a staff station.

Towards the end of the independent days Carisbrooke was abandoned as a passing loop and both up and down trains used the Down loop, the signals out of use having wooden crosses nailed on the arms, while the driver carried both the Newport to Carisbrooke, and Carisbrooke to Ningwood staffs.

Yarmouth was later abandoned as a passing place, but here the formality of using the signals was not considered necessary and down trains were admitted to the up loop by a green hand signal from the signal box!

The long and short staff section was worked by the SR on the branch, Ningwood, the passing place, being cut out as a crossing as required. The Sykes old pattern two semaphore instrument with short staff and ticket was still used, with Ningwood as a crossing place, but when Ningwood was cut out the long staff was carried by the driver.

When the FYN company began to work their own line in 1913, the block was transferred from Newport North signal box to the Freshwater company's Newport box, so that there were no instruments between Newport FYN box and Newport North IWC box. So when trains started to work through again in 1920, the 'block' between the two signal boxes consisted of the FYN signalman walking to the end of the platform and shouting to the Newport North signalman, 'Train on from Calbourne, George'.

Appendix III

GRADIENTS
RYDE PIER HEAD AND VENTNOR

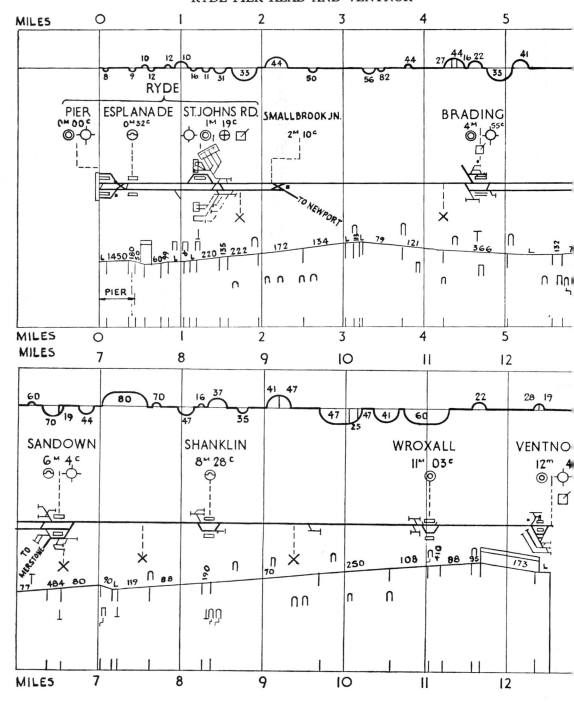

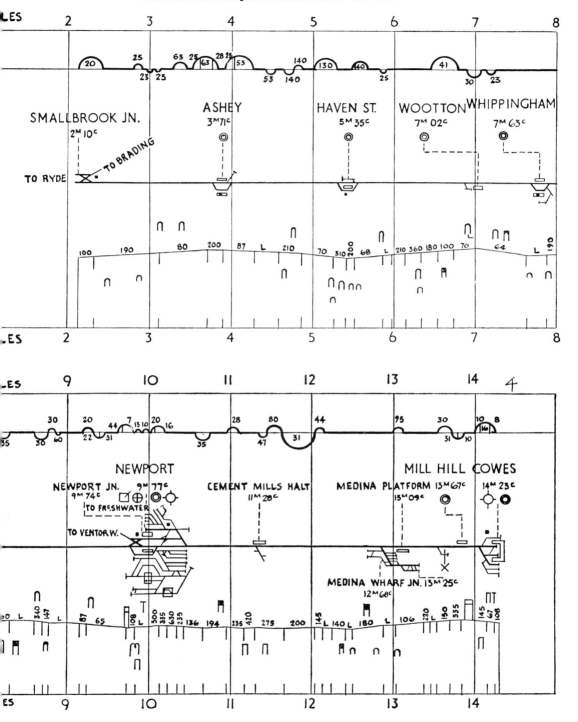

NEWPORT JUNCTION AND FRESHWATER

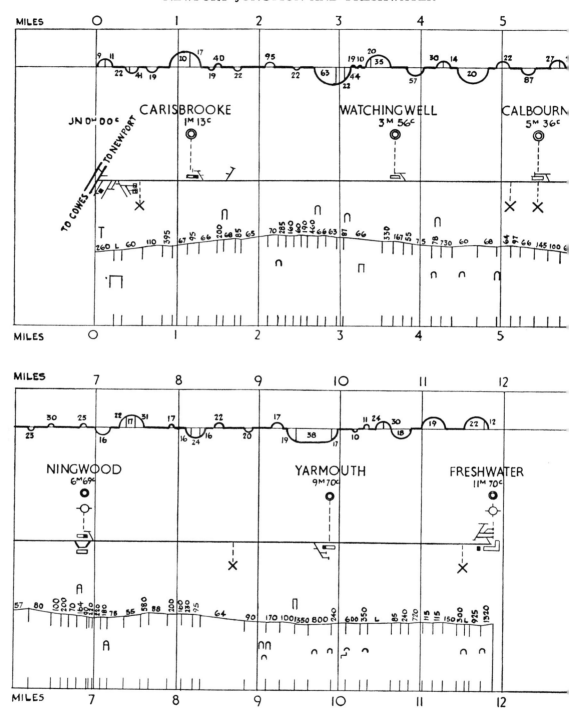

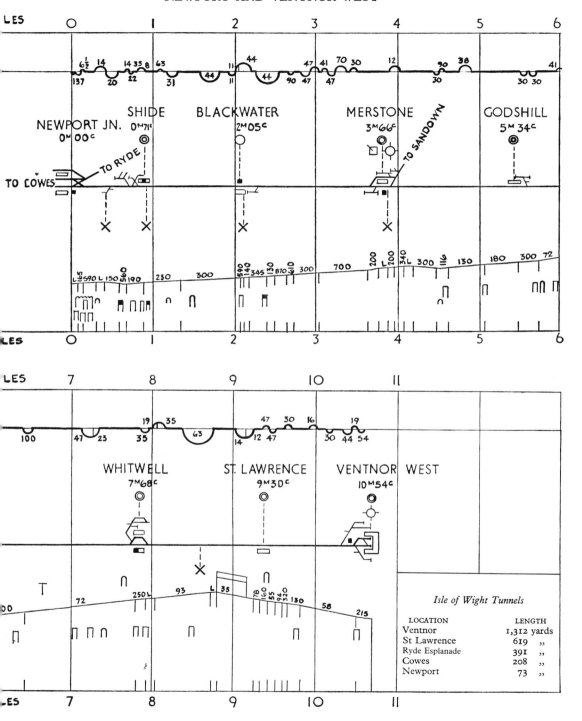

Isle of Wight Tunnels

LOCATION	LENGTH
Ventnor	1,312 yards
St Lawrence	619 ,,
Ryde Esplanade	391 ,,
Cowes	208 ,,
Newport	73 ,,

SANDOWN AND MERSTONE JUNCTION

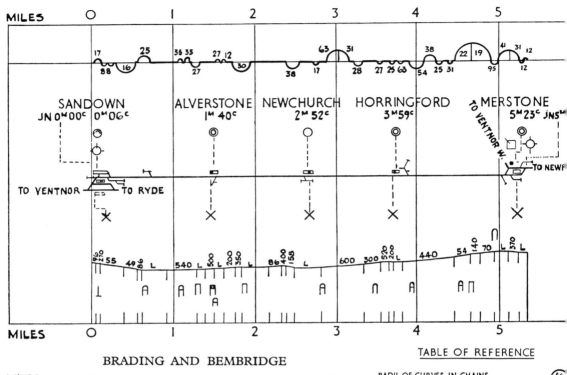

MILES 0 1 2 3 4 5

SANDOWN
JN 0ᴹ00ᶜ 0ᴹ06ᶜ

ALVERSTONE
1ᴹ40ᶜ

NEWCHURCH
2ᴹ52ᶜ

HORRINGFORD
3ᴹ59ᶜ

MERSTONE
5ᴹ23ᶜ JNSᴹ

TO VENTNOR W.

TO NEWP

TO VENTNOR   TO RYDE

MILES 0 1 2 3 4 5

BRADING AND BEMBRIDGE

MILES 0 1 2 3

BRADING
0ᴹ00ᶜ

ST. HELENS
1ᴹ55ᶜ

BEMBRIDGE
2ᴹ65ᶜ

TO RYDE

TO SANDOWN

MILES 0 1 2 3

TABLE OF REFERENCE

RADII OF CURVES IN CHAINS............... 56
BRICK BUILT STATIONS...................
BRICK & TIMBER BUILT STATIONS...........
TIMBER BUILT STATIONS..................
WATERING STATIONS......................
ENGINE SHEDS ....
ENGINE TURNTABLES......................
COALING STATIONS.......................
ELECTRIC POWER STATIONS................
SIGNAL BOXES...........................
BRIDGE NUMBERS.........................45
MILE POSTS ....
PUBLIC ROAD LEVEL-CROSSINGS............
MILEAGE GIVEN THUS 89ᴹ56ᶜREVISION
                          MILEAGE

GRADIENTS ....264 OR 264
W.I. OR STEEL BRIDGES..................
W.I. OR STEEL & BRICK BRIDGES..........
C.I. BRIDGES...........................
C.I. & BRICK BRIDGES...................
TIMBER BRIDGES.........................
BRICK ARCHES & SUBWAYS.................
CULVERTS...............................
REINFORCED CONCRETE BRIDGES...........
STEEL FOOTBRIDGES......................
TIMBER FOOTBRIDGES.....................
STEEL FOOT-SUBWAYS.....................
TUNNELS................................
DIVISIONAL OR COUNTY BOUNDARIES........ KENT
                                        SURREY

Appendix IV

RYDE PIER TRAMWAY

The Ryde Pier tramway was built as long ago as 1863 to connect the steam-boats at the Pier Head with the shore. It opened with horse traction in 1864 at the same time as the IWR; later it was connected up, via the streets of the little town to St John's Road station making its total length 1¼ miles. In 1864, before the line was opened to the public, a small Manning Wardle 0-4-0 saddle tank (No. 111) was tried on the pier with Mr Wardle, no less, at the controls but it was not successful. In 1876 a Merryweather steam tram engine, presumably a 0-4-0 was tried for some months but it too did not find favour. Meanwhile the joint LBSC/LSWR lines from St John's Road and the new railway pier were going forward and the new through line opened to Esplanade on April 5, 1880 and to the Pier Head on July 12th. The tram through the streets ultimately ceased. The separate pier railway continued in spite of this and before it went over to electric traction in March 1886 it gave a prolonged trial of steam locomotion between January 1881 and November 1884 with two tramway engines supplied by Bradleys of Kidderminster. Originally these engines had been designed to burn gas but this turned out to be unsatisfactory and a gas-holder built at the pier foot was removed. These engines are reported as having been sold to the Ryde Gas Co. in October 1886 so it is not clear whether they or one of them worked on the Freshwater line or not; the dates quoted would make it possible. The Ryde Pier Railway was taken over by the Southern Railway in 1924 who abandoned electric traction in 1927 and replaced the electric cars with two Drewry petrol railcars. This very essential tramway and its machines are now in the stock of British Railways and a rare mess Island transport would be without them.

RELEVANT DATES

1812	Ryde Pier Company formed.
1814	Ryde Pier opened (1,740 ft)[1]
	Passengers walked from ship to Ryde.
June 3, 1857	Ryde Pier Company Board of Directors perused a report issued by a Mr Walker (of Messrs Walker, Burges & Cooper of 3 Great George Street) suggesting there should be 'a line of railway drawn by a locomotive or a horse' on the Pier.
March 30, 1861	The Board resolved that a tramway be made and Mr Cooper of Messrs Walker, Burges & Cooper was asked to reconsider the plan of 1857.
April 7, 1862	Messrs Langdon were appointed contractors for the tramway.
June 1, 1863	The Board decided upon the type of carriage to be used. Two vehicles, one for passengers, and one light luggage van, 13 feet long with brake power, should be provided.
June 5, 1863	Seats on the roof were suggested.
October 3, 1863	The Board fixed the fares as 3d 1st class and 2d 2nd class.
October 17, 1863	Method of traction was discussed.
November 7, 1863	Messrs Manning Wardle & Co. were asked to supply 'a small locomotive engine, 6″ cylinder and 12″ stroke, in working trim, 6½ tons, sufficient to move a gross load of 96 tons on the level'. The locomotive to be sent for trial, with the option of return to the firm after three months.
January 9, 1864	Provision of a temporary engine shed was discussed.
March 19, 1864	The Board were advised that the engine had been tried out on two occasions, and there was some slight vibration to the Pier as temporary track had been laid. The opening ceremony was to be postponed 'for the present'.
May 4, 1864	The engine was returned to the makers. A Mr Ayshford of Walham Green was asked to see the Directors about a saloon omnibus for the tramway.
June 20, 1864	Mr Ayshford was commissioned to build a bus.
July 16, 1864	The Board decided that the 1st class fare should be 4d.
September 3, 1864	Although the new bus was apparently damaged in the crossing, it was repaired and used, drawn by a horse and a service started.
May 1865	The Board mentioned a second carriage might be required.
November 2, 1865	The Board resolved to apply for power 'to extend the tramway from the southern terminus to the Ryde station of the Isle of Wight Railway (St John's Road). This and further applications were rejected in 1866.
1869	The Pier Company received the required authority by the Ryde Pier Railways Extension Act of 1870.

June 5, 1869	Contract was made for the first portion along the Esplanade to Messrs Langdon who completed the work in 1870.
September 24, 1870	Contract was also made for the second portion from Esplanade to St John's Road with Coker, who completed it in 1871.
August 1, 1871	The tramway extension was opened and a service operated. IWR vans were also hauled over the tramway to the Pier Head by horses.
1872	A spur line was begun from the tramway to the basin at the end of Victoria Pier, which was opened for goods traffic in 1873.
June 1876	The Directors agreed to hire a steam engine from Merryweathers for use on the Pier itself (but not on the extension to Ryde St John's Road owing to local opposition).
September 29, 1876	Merryweather steam tram engine arrived for trials (after a short period test on the Southsea Tramways). The Mayor and Corporation were present at the trial and although pleased with the performance considered it made excessive smoke.
December 1876	The engine was returned to the makers on instructions from the Board.
July 1879	The Board considered other forms of traction, such as wire rope haulage, or a car driven by a gas-fired steam engine, which a Mr Bradley of Kidderminster could supply.
February 21, 1880	Mr F. Bradley of Glenmore Works, Kidderminster undertook to fit two of the tramcars with machinery for propelling them with steam generated by gas heat, and to take the apparatus back after a reasonable time if the trams did not work satisfactorily. The Ryde Gas Company undertook to provide sufficient gas pressure to fill the bag or bellows required for working these engines, and a small gas-holder was to be placed at the Pier Toll Gate station.
March 27, 1880	The contract was made with Mr Bradley. (See note [2].)
November 27, 1880	The Directors were not satisfied, and Mr Bradley agreed to convert the tramcar engines from gas furnaces to coke.
January 7, 1881	The two steam tram engines arrived.
February 12, 1881	One was working on the Pier, in perfect order.

After numerous teething troubles, the trams settled down and worked the services till October 31, 1884, when they were withdrawn owing to bad condition. (See note [3].)

November 1, 1884	Horse traction was resumed.
October 1885	The Directors gave a contract to Messrs Siemens of Charlton to electrify the Pier tramway, and work was started at once to lay an electric pick up rail on the double track. A gas engine and dynamo were installed in a building at the Pier Toll Gate for generating the current. (Later this plant was doubled.) The extension from Pier Gates to Ryde St John's Road was probably uprooted at this period.
March 1886	Electric traction commenced with two single deck motor cars and two of the old horse trams, converted to single deck, as trailers.
October 1886	The two Bradley steam tram locomotives were sold to the Ryde Gas Company.
1924	The Southern Railway acquired the Ryde Pier Company under its act of 1924, but maintained the electric trams for the next three years.
November 1927	The SR condemned the electric traction and introduced two new four-wheeled Drewry railcars, with 26 h.p. Bedford engines, two of the electric trailers were retained, including the famous 'Grapes' car. A flat truck was coupled to one of the sets for conveying luggage.
1936, 1937	Two new trailer cars were built to match the Drewry cars and the old trailers were withdrawn, the 'Grapes' car being sent to the Hull Transport Museum for preservation. This vehicle had been built in Ryde by a carpenter named Knapp, in the horse days, from solid mahogany and was originally painted vermilion with blue panelling, purple grapes and the interior gilded, mats were also put on the platforms for wiping the feet.

NOTES TO APPENDIX IV

[1] Subsequently the Pier was extended as the tramway was ultimately 700 yards long.

[2] The LSW & LBSC Joint Railway was opened on July 12, 1880 from St John's Road beside the tramway extension route, and under the town by a tunnel surfacing at the Esplanade end of Ryde Pier, and proceeding on a new pier alongside the tramway to the Pier Head (an intermediate railway station was built called Ryde Esplanade at the Pier Gates), so that now the IWR trains could go up to the Pier Head.

[3] A friend of one of the authors, the late Mr S. Y. Knight, who was a pupil at Longhedge Works of the London Chatham & Dover Railway under Mr W. Kirtley, remembers one of these engines on the Pier. It had a vertical boiler, with the engine driving a centre jackshaft, which was coupled by side rods to the four-coupled wheels. The reversing gear was by means of a wheel at each end of the vehicle, which operated the valve travel. One reason for withdrawal was the fear of cinders dropping from the ashpan and setting the Pier alight. Although the whole of each side had wooden louvres above the waist-line, he adds, the engine was 'infernally' hot, as he frequently rode in it.

118. Double and single decker horse trams on Ryde Pier, between 1871–8

119. The famous 'Grapes' car which ran behind horse, steam, electric and petrol motive power. It is now in Hull Museum

120. Merryweather steam tram locomotive in Ryde Pier trials in 1876

121. Drewry petrol car and old trailer

Appendix V

STEAMERS

(A) Portsmouth & Ryde Steam Packet Company, later Portsmouth & Ryde Joint Stock Steam Packet Company 1825–1851

Built	Acquired	Name	Type	Builders	Length	Breadth	Depth	Gross Tons	Remarks	Broken Up
1822	Bought 1825	Union	Wood, Paddle, Steam	W. Evans, Rotherhithe	87.25ft	11.0ft	7.5ft	54	1851 to PPRUSP Co.	1863
1823	Bought 1827	Arrow	Wood, Paddle, Steam	J. Lang, Dumbarton	92.8ft	11.9ft	7.0ft	46		1833
1826	1826	Lord Yarborough	Wood, Paddle, Steam	D. List, Fishbourne I.W.	88.8ft	14.3ft	9.5ft	54	Sold 1852	1868
1835	1835	Earl Spencer	Wood, Paddle, Steam	B. Denham, Ryde I.W.	85.8ft	12.0ft	7.8ft	43	1851 to PPRUSP Co. Sold 1855	1858
1847	1847	Prince Albert	Wood, Paddle, Steam	G. & J. Inman, Southampton	96.0ft	12.4ft	8.1ft	61	1851 to PPRUSP Co.	1871
1850	1850	Her Majesty	Iron, Paddle, Steam	Robinson Russell, Millwall	129.1ft	14.0ft	7.2ft	75	1851 to PPRUSP Co.	1879

(B) Portsea, Portsmouth, Gosport & Isle of Wight New Steam Packet Company 1850–1851

Built	Acquired	Name	Type	Builders	Length	Breadth	Depth	Gross Tons	Remarks	Broken Up
1850	1850	Prince of Wales	Wood, Paddle, Steam	J. White, East Cowes, I.W.	107.6ft	13.2ft	8.3ft	87	1851 to PPRUSP Co.	1876
1850	1850	Princess Royal	Wood, Paddle, Steam	J. White, East Cowes, I.W.	107.6ft	13.2ft	8.3ft	87	1851 to PPRUSP Co.	1876

(C) Port of Portsmouth & Ryde United Steam Packet Company Limited [Amalgamation of A & B 1851] 1851–1880

Built	Acquired	Name	Type	Builders	Length	Breadth	Depth	Gross Tons	Remarks	Broken Up
1859	1859	Prince Consort	Iron, Paddle, Steam	J. Scott Russell, Millwall	154.5ft	15.1ft	6.7ft	104	1880 to LSWR & LBSCR Joint	1882
1865	1865	Princess of Wales	Iron, Paddle, Steam	Lewis, London	152.4ft	16.0ft	6.9ft	150	1880 to LSWR & LBSCR Joint, converted to hulk 1885	
1869	1869	Duke of Edinburgh	Iron, Paddle, Steam	Money Wigram & Son, Blackwall	136.1ft	14.0ft	7.0ft	95	1880 to LSWR & LBSCR Joint	1884
1869	1869	Princess Alice	Iron, Paddle, Steam		136.2ft	14.1ft	7.0ft	95	1880 to LSWR & LBSCR Joint	1892
1873	1873	Princess Louise	Iron, Screw, Steam	Lewis & Stockwell, Blackwall	103.6ft	17.0ft	6.6ft	111	Sold 1874, renamed Jennie 1875, sold Greek 1904	
1874	1874	Princess Beatrice	Iron, Screw, Steam	Lewis & Stockwell, E. Greenwich	103.6ft	17.0ft	6.6ft	99	Sold 1874 to HM Consul in Martinique	
1871	Bought 1875	Heather Bell	Iron, Paddle, Steam	Blackwood & Gordon, Pt. Glasgow	207.7ft	21.0ft	8.8ft	271	Sold 1900, and eventually to South Coast & Continental S. Ltd. Southampton	1902
1878	1878	Albert Edward	Iron, Paddle, Steam	Oswald, Mordawnt & Co., Southampton	169.4ft	20.5ft	9.0ft	269	1880 to LSWR & LBSCR Joint. Sold 1893 to David Macbrayne, renamed Carabinier	
1879	1879	Alexandra	Iron, Paddle, Steam	Scott & Co., Greenock	171.0ft	20.2ft	8.5ft	235	1880 to LSWR & LBSCR Joint. Sold 1913 to Bembridge & Seaview SP Co.	1934

Southsea & Isle of Wight Steam Ferry Company. 1873 Sold to PPRUSP Co. Ltd. 1877 (C)

Built	Acquired	Name	Type	Builders	Length	Breadth	Depth	Gross Tons	Remarks	Broken Up
1873	1873	Ryde (II)	Wood, Screw, Steam	J. S. White, Cowes I.W.	99.4ft	16.2ft	7.1ft	59	Sold circa 1878	1897
1873	1873	Shanklin (II)	Wood, Screw, Steam	J. S. White, Cowes I.W.	99.2ft	16.4ft	7.1ft	63	Sold circa 1880 Registered in London 1905	
1873	1873	Ventnor	Wood, Screw, Steam	J. S. White, Cowes I.W.	90.0ft	16.1ft	7.3ft	51	Sold circa 1878 Stranded 1893	1907
1873	1873	Southsea (I)	Wood, Screw, Steam	S.I.W.S.F. Co., Portsmouth	97.0ft	15.8ft	6.8ft	71	Sold circa 1880	

London & South Western and London Brighton & South Coast Railway Companies 1880–1922

Built	Acquired	Name	Type	Builders	Length	Breadth	Depth	Gross Tons	Remarks	Broken Up
1881	1881	Victoria	Steel, Paddle, Steam	Aitken & Mansel	191.9ft	25.1ft	8.6ft	366	Sold 1899 to SIW SERMSP Co., then to Holland 1900	1900
1884	1884	Duchess of Edinburgh	Steel, Paddle, Steam	Aitken & Mansel	190.6ft	26.1ft	8.8ft	342	Sold 1910. Double-ended, funnels athwartships	1910
1884	1884	Duchess of Connaught	Steel, Paddle, Steam	Aitken & Mansel	190.6ft	26.1ft	8.8ft	342	Sold 1910. Double-ended, funnels athwartships	1910
*1889	1889	Duchess of Albany	Steel, Paddle, Steam	Scott & Co., Greenock	170.4ft	22.1ft	8.5ft	256	1923 to SR Sold 1925 to Holland	1928
*1893	1893	Princess Margaret	Steel, Paddle, Steam	Scott & Co., Greenock	170.6ft	22.1ft	8.5ft	260	1923 to SR Sold 1928 to Holland	1928

*Stokes Bay Ferry

The Isle of Wight Ferry Company of 1856 was closely allied to the Stokes Bay Railway Company of 1855 and both were independent undertakings. A short branch line was built from Gosport on the L.S.W.R. to a new pier at Stokes Bay to accommodate a ferry service to Ryde, at all states of the tide. The line and pier were opened in 1863 and were worked by the L.S.W.R. The Ferry Company operated the service with three ships named "Chancellor", "Gareloch" and "Victoria"; the former having been built in 1853 and the two other ships in 1860 in either the north of England or the Clyde. No other details have come to light. In 1872 the line, pier and ferry were leased to the L.S.W.R. for 999 years, and the whole undertaking was finally acquired in 1875 by the Railway Company. The L.S.W.R. & L.B.S.C.R. joint steamers "Duchess of Albany" and "Princess Margaret" worked the service in the latter years until the closure for passenger traffic in 1913. The branch line south of Gosport Road station and the pier were sold to the Admiralty in 1922.

Built	Name	Construction	Builder	Length	Beam	Draught	Tonnage	Notes	Disposed
1899	Duchess of Fife	Steel, Paddle, Steam	Clydebank E. S. B. Co. Ltd.	215.0ft	26.1ft	9.5ft	443	SP Co., renamed *Clacton Queen* 1923 to SR Sold 1929	1929
1910	Duchess of Richmond	Steel, Paddle, Steam	D. & W. Henderson Co. Ltd., Glasgow	190.0ft	26.1ft	8.7ft	354	Sunk by striking mine 1915	
1911	Duchess of Norfolk	Steel, Paddle, Steam	D. & W. Henderson Co. Ltd., Glasgow	190.0ft	26.1ft	8.7ft	381	1923 to SR – Sold 1937 to Cosens Ltd., Weymouth, renamed *Embassy*	

†Isle of Wight Marine Transit Company Ltd. 1884 [Taken over by LB&SCR in 1886]

Built	Name	Construction	Builder	Length	Beam	Draught	Tonnage	Notes	Disposed
1858	Carrier	Iron, Paddle, Steam	Scott & Co., Greenock	124.4ft	26.7ft	8.5ft	243	Bought from North British Railway	1890

Southern Railway Company. Portsmouth Section 1923–1947

Built	Name	Construction	Builder	Length	Beam	Draught	Tonnage	Notes	Disposed
1924	Shanklin (II)	Steel, Paddle, Steam	J. I. Thornycroft Ltd., Southampton	190.0ft	26.1ft	8.7ft	412	Sold 1951 to Cosens Ltd., renamed *Monarch* (II)	1961
1928	Portsdown	Steel, Paddle, Steam	Caledon S. & E. Co., Dundee	190.0ft	25.1ft	8.7ft	342	Sunk by striking mine 1941 (on normal service)	
1928	Merstone	Steel, Paddle, Steam	Caledon S. & E. Co., Dundee	190.0ft	25.1ft	8.7ft	342	Sunk by striking mine 1941	1952
1930	Whippingham	Steel, Paddle, Steam	Fairfield S. & E. Co. Ltd., Govan	244.0ft	30.1ft	10.5ft	825		
1930	Southsea (II)	Steel, Paddle, Steam	Fairfield S. & E. Co. Ltd., Govan	244.0ft	30.1ft	10.5ft	825		
1934	Sandown	Steel, Paddle, Steam	Wm Denny & Bros. Ltd.	216.0ft	29.1ft	10.0ft	684		
1937	Ryde (II)	Steel, Paddle, Steam	Wm Denny & Bros. Ltd.	220.0ft	29.0ft	10.5ft	566		

[Portsmouth – Fishbourne Car Ferry Service]

Built	Name	Construction	Builder	Length	Beam	Draught	Tonnage	Notes	Disposed
1927	Fishbourne	Steel, Screw, Diesel	Wm Denny & Bros. Ltd.	118.0ft	25.1ft	7.2ft	136	Became *Fishbourne* (II), laid up 1961	
1928	Wootton	Steel, Screw, Diesel	Wm Denny & Bros. Ltd.	121.0ft	26.1ft	7.7ft	149	Laid up 1961	
1930	Hilsea	Steel, Screw, Diesel	Wm Denny & Bros. Ltd.	121.0ft	26.1ft	7.7ft	149	Laid up 1961	

British Railways (Southern Region) [Portsmouth Section] 1948–

Built	Name	Construction	Builder	Length	Beam	Draught	Tonnage	Notes	Disposed
1948	Southsea (III)	Steel, Screw, Diesel	Wm. Denny & Bros. Ltd.	200.0ft	48.0ft	7.0ft	837		
1948	Brading	Steel, Screw, Diesel	Wm. Denny & Bros. Ltd.	200.0ft	48.0ft	7.0ft	837		
1951	Shanklin (III)	Steel, Screw, Diesel	Wm. Denny & Bros. Ltd.	200.0ft	48.0ft	7.0ft	833		

Portsmouth – Fishbourne Car Ferry Service

Built	Name	Construction	Builder	Length	Beam	Draught	Tonnage	Notes	Disposed
1961	Fishbourne (II)	Steel, Screw, Diesel		166.0ft	43.0ft	6.0ft	293		
1961	Camber Queen	Steel, Screw, Diesel		166.0ft	43.0ft	6.0ft	293		
1983	St Catherine	Steel, Voith-Schneider diesel		76.94m	16.8m	2.451m	2,036		
1983	St Helen	Steel, Voith-Schneider diesel		76.94m	16.8m	2.451m	2,983		

Solent Steamship Company Ltd [George Grunsell, Lymington]

Built	Name	Construction	Builder	Length	Beam	Draught	Tonnage	Notes	Disposed
1856	Red Lion	Wood, Paddle, Steam	North Shields	76.8ft	15.7ft	8.3ft	54	1884 to LSWR Sold 1901	1880
1863	Solent (II)	Wood, Paddle, Steam	Lymington	94.0ft	15.6ft	7.1ft	61	1884 to LSWR	1901
1866	Mayflower	Wood, Paddle, Steam	Newcastle	98.3ft	15.7ft	6.8ft	69		1910

London & South Western Region Railway Company. (Absorbed Solent Steamship Co. 1884)

Built	Name	Construction	Builder	Length	Beam	Draught	Tonnage	Notes	Disposed
1893	Lymington (I)	Steel, Paddle, Steam	Day, Summers Co., Southampton	120.2ft	18.1ft	7.7ft	130	Sold 1927, renamed *Glengarry*, later sold as training ship for navy cadets as *Lord Nelson*	
1902	Solent (III)	Steel, Paddle, Steam	Mordey, Carney Ltd.,	133.5ft	20.2ft	7.7ft	161	Sold 1948, became roadside café at Porchester	

†*The Isle of Wight Marine Transit Company*

The Isle of Wight Marine Transit Company was formed in 1884 to instal and operate a train ferry between Langstone Harbour on the L.B. & S.C.R. Hayling Island branch and St. Helen's in Brading Harbour with connection to the Isle of Wight Railway, a distance of eleven miles. After the opening of the Forth Bridge, one of the North British Railway train ferries, which had conveyed railway wagons between Granton and Burntisland, became redundant and was bought by the Marine Transit Company to operate the new service. This vessel named "Carrier" had two lines of rail on the train deck and these were used to carry one line of seven loaded wagons, with seven empties on the other track. The service commenced in 1885, and the company was sold to the L.B. & S.C.R. in 1886 after one year's operation, but the heavy seas frequently encountered in crossing Spithead proved more than the "Carrier" had been designed to cope with; so the service was terminated in 1888. The "Carrier" was broken up in 1890.

A rather amusing story is told of the perky little "Carrier" belching forth black smoke when sailing along the line at one of the Spithead Naval Reviews, immediately in front of the Royal Yacht. The indignity of the preceding "Carrier" caused much annoyance to the Royal Personage on board; consequently the Naval Authorities were careful in the future to prohibit the area, during Naval Reviews, to all other than Naval craft.

Built	Acquired	Name	Type	Builders	Length	Breadth	Depth	Gross Tons	Remarks	Broken Up
1927	1927	Freshwater (II)	Steel, Paddle, Steam	J. S. White, Cowes I.W.	152.5ft	23.1ft	8.3ft	263	Sold 1960, renamed Freshwater (II) by BR Became Sussex Queen, later Swanage Queen	1962
1938	1938	Lymington (III)	Steel, Screw, Diesel	Wm. Denny & Bros. Ltd.	132.2ft	26.1ft	8.1ft	275	Voith-Schneider propulsion. Car ferry	
1947	1948	Farringford	Steel, Paddle, Diesel	Wm. Denny & Bros. Ltd.	162.2ft	28.1ft	8.6ft	489	Diesel-Electric. Car ferry	
1959	1959	Freshwater (III)	Steel, Screw, Diesel	Ailsa Shipbldg Co., Troon	164.0ft	43.0ft	6.0ft	363	Voith-Schneider propulsion. Car ferry	
		Southampton, Isle of Wight and Portsmouth Improved Steamboat Co. Amalgamated with the SIW & SERMSP Co. in 1864								
1861	1861	Lord of the Islas	Iron, Paddle, Steam	Thames Steamboat Co., London	147.6ft	17.9ft	7.6ft	104		1890
1861	1861	Lady of the Lake	Iron, Paddle, Steam	Thames Steamboat Co., London	145.0ft	18.1ft	6.6ft	126		1888
		Southampton, Isle of Wight and South of England Royal Mail Steam Packet Co Ltd 1861 [Red Funnel Line 1935]								
1852	1852	Medina (I)	Wood, Paddle, Steam	J. White, Cowes, I.W.	120.8ft	14.9ft	8.6ft	104	The last ship from one of the original companies	1983
1866	1866	Vectis	Wood, Paddle, Steam	J. White, Cowes, I.W	140.7ft	18.2ft	8.2ft	122	Converted to cargo vessel, circa 1896	1912
1872	1872	Southampton	Iron, Paddle, Steam	Barclay Curle & Co., Glasgow	150.1ft	20.1ft	8.7ft	203	Sold 1902, became St. Elian	1915
1876	1876	Carisbrooke	Iron, Paddle, Steam	Barclay Curle & Co., Glasgow	165.7ft	20.1ft	8.0ft	198	Sold 1905, became Rhostrevor/St. Trillo /San Telmo	1932
1876	1876	Prince Leopold	Iron, Paddle, Steam	Barclay Curle & Co., Glasgow	165.6ft	20.1ft	7.9ft	196	Sold 1905, became Rhosneigr wrecked 1908	
1880	1880	Princess Beatrice	Iron, Paddle, Steam	Barclay Curle & Co., Glasgow	175.7ft	20.1ft	8.2ft	253	Sold 1933 to Pollock, Brown & Co. for scrapping	1933
1883	1883	Princess Helena	Iron, Paddle, Steam	Barclay Curle & Co., Glasgow	175.4ft	20.2ft	8.3ft	246	Converted to car ferry 1927, sunk in Air Raid Southampton 1940	1952
1885	1885	Her Majesty	Iron, Paddle, Steam	Barclay Curle & Co., Glasgow	185.2ft	20.1ft	8.3ft	325		
1889	1889	Solent Queen (I)	Steel, Paddle, Steam	Southampton Naval Works	215.6ft	21.1ft	8.2ft	324		1948
1891	1891	Prince of Wales	Steel, Paddle, Steam	Barclay Curle & Co., Glasgow	185.5ft	22.2ft	7.5ft	280		1938
1896	1896	Duchess of York/ Cornwall	Steel, Paddle, Steam	Barclay Curle & Co., Glasgow	185.5ft	22.1ft	8.6ft	302	Renamed 1928, converted to car ferry 1947	1950
1898	1898	Lorna Doone (I)	Steel, Paddle, Steam	Napier, Shanks & Bell, Glasgow	220.5ft	26.0ft	9.2ft	427	Purchased from J. Gunn, Cardiff	1946
1881	1899	Victoria	Steel, Paddle, Steam	Aitken & Mansel	191.9ft	25.1ft	8.6ft	366	Purchased from LSWR & LBSCR Joint Fleet (double-ender)	1900
1900	1900	Balmoral (I)	Steel, Paddle, Steam	S. McKnight & Co., Ayr	236.0ft	27.1ft	9.6ft	473	First renamed 1936; again renamed Corfe Castle 1937 to clear name for the new Cunard liner	1946
1902	1902	Queen (II)/Mauretania	Steel, Paddle, Steam	J. Reid & Son, Glasgow	200.3ft	24.1ft	8.3ft	345		1938
1899	1907	Stirling Castle	Steel, Paddle, Steam	J. Scott & Co., Kinghorn	170.0ft	24.2ft	7.6ft	271	Purchased from Galloway Saloon SP Co. 1907, sunk minesweeping 1916	
1908	1908	Bournemouth Queen	Steel, Paddle, Steam	Ailsa Shipbuilding Co., Troon	200.1ft	24.1ft	8.0ft	353	Purchased from B&SCSP 1909, converted cargo vessel 1911	1957
1876	1909	Lord Elgin	Iron, Paddle, Steam	Richardson, Duck & Co., Stockton	160.0ft	20.0ft	6.8ft	203		1955
1911	1911	Princess Mary	Steel, Paddle, Steam	Day, Summers & Co., Southampton	195.2ft	24.1ft	8.1ft	326	Wrecked on war service in Dardanelles 1919	
1927	1927	Princess Elizabeth	Steel, Paddle, Steam	Day, Summers & Co., Southampton	195.0ft	24.2ft	8.0ft	388	Sold to Torbay Steamers Ltd. 1959	
1931	1931	Medina (III)	Steel, Screw, Diesel	J. I. Thornycroft & Co., Southampton	143.1ft	28.1ft	8.7ft	342	Sold to M. H. Bland, Gibraltar 1962, renamed Mons Abyla	
1936	1936	Gracie Fields	Steel, Paddle, Steam	J. I. Thornycroft & Co., Southampton	195.9ft	24.9ft	8.0ft	393	Sunk at Dunkirk 1940	
1939	1939	Vecta	Steel, Screw, Diesel	J. I. Thornycroft & Co., Southampton	199.5ft	30.2ft	8.7ft	630	Diesel Electric, twin screw 1946 (originally Voith-Schneider propulsion)	
1925	1946	Upton	Steel, Screw, Steam	Cammell Laird & Co. Ltd.	145.1ft	32.0ft	11.4ft	462	Bought from Birkenhead Corporation, ex Mersey Ferry	1953
1914	1948	Robina	Steel, Screw, Steam	Ardrossan Dockyard & S.B. Co.	159.6ft	26.1ft	8.8ft	306	Bought from Coast Lines Ltd.	1953
1943	1948	Norris Castle	Steel, Screw, Diesel	Alex Findlay	186.0ft	38.1ft	6.7ft	473	Ex Landing Craft Tanks. Car ferry bow loading. Built as minesweeper HMS Atherstone	

		Name	Construction	Builder	Length	Beam	Depth	Tonnage	Notes	
1916	1949	*Lorna Doone (II)*	Steel, Paddle, Steam	Ailsa Shipbuilding Co., Troon	235.2ft	23.0ft	9.2ft	738	Bought from New Medway SP Co. as *Queen of Kent*. Built as minesweeper HMS *Melton*	
1916	1949	*Solent Queen (II)*	Steel, Paddle, Steam	W. Hamilton & Co., Glasgow	235.2ft	29.0ft	9.2ft	832	Bought from New Medway SP Co. as *Queen of Thanet*	1951
1949		*Balmoral (II)*	Steel, Screw, Diesel	J. I. Thornycroft & Co., Southampton	195.7ft	30.1ft	8.9ft	688	Car ferry, end or side loading	
1959		*Carisbrooke Castle*	Steel, Screw, Diesel	J. I. Thornycroft & Co., Southampton	191.2ft	40.0ft		671	Car ferry, end or side loading	
1962		*Osborne Castle*	Steel, Screw, Diesel	J. I. Thornycroft & Co., Southampton	188.3ft	42.1ft		730		
Southsea & Ventnor Steamship Company (F. M. Coldwell)										
1878	1886	*Princess of Wales/ Bembridge*	Iron, Paddle, Steam	London Steamboat Co.	137.4ft	16.1ft	6.8ft	104	Bought from London SB Co., renamed *Bembridge*. Sold to S. Wheeler, Southsea, Ventnor, Shanklin & Sandown S. Co. 1896	1913
1878	1892	*Island Queen*	Iron, Paddle, Steam	Port Glasgow	125.1ft	15.1ft	6.1ft	97	Completed in 1882 for Mrs A. Freeman, Southsea. Sold to S&VS Co. 1892. Sold to Algeciras (Gibraltar) Rly Co. in 1898	
1881	1897	*Winnie*	Iron, Paddle, Steam	Freckleton, Lancs	90.0ft	14.1ft	6.1ft	54	Bought from SVS&SS Co. 1897	1912
Southsea, Ventnor, Shanklin & Sandown Steamship Company (Samuel Wheeler)										
1866	1888	*Dandie Dinmont*	Iron, Paddle, Steam	A. & J. Inglis	197.2ft	22.1ft	6.9ft	215	Bought from North British SP Co. Sank in Portsmouth Harbour in 1901. Sold foreign for breaking up.	1902
Bembridge and Seaview Steam Packet Company										
1879	1913	*Alexandra*	Iron, Paddle, Steam	Scott & Co., Greenock	171.0ft	20.2ft	8.5ft	235	Bought from LSWR & LBSCR Joint Companies, then sold to Cosens & Co. also in 1913	1934
1914		*Alleyn*	Paddle, Steam	Thames Ironworks	130.0ft	18.0ft	6.8ft	116		

122. P.S. *Ryde* the last paddle survivor, 1966

123. P.S. *Lorna Doone* of the Southampton fleet, distinguished in two wars

124. One of the 'Duchesses' of the SW & SCR fleet

125. Train ferry used in the eighties between Langstone and St. Helens. (see page 121)

126. P.S. *Whippingham* one of the biggest built for this service

127. The last ship added for the Portsmouth–Ryde service, the M.V. *Shanklin*

MOTORING IN THE ISLE OF WIGHT.

Loading Motor Cars at Lymington.

NO Motor Tour through England can be considered complete which does not include a run round the Isle of Wight (sixty miles). The most convenient point for crossing is at Lymington, on the South side of the charming New Forest, where the London and South Western Railway Company has provided efficient accommodation for such traffic, including slipways whereby cars can be shipped by their own power, on to specially constructed boats, thus entirely obviating the necessity of lifting, and removing a difficulty which hitherto has deterred many from visiting the lovely "Garden Isle."

The boats—towed by fast, powerful tugs—quickly negotiate the passage, which is the shortest and most sheltered, to the island. On Week-days (weather and circumstances permitting) the boats leave Lymington Town Station Wharf at 9*30, 11.30 a.m., 2.30 and 4.45 p.m. for Yarmouth, and leave Yarmouth at 8.*0 a.m., 12.30, 3.15 and 5.30 p.m. for Lymington. Cars should be upon the Wharf half-an-hour before these times.

* Prior notice should be given to the Station Master at Lymington in regard to conveyance by these boats.

Special passages can be arranged on Sundays upon arrangement being made with the Station Master, Lymington (Telephone No. 7), not later than the previous day, the extra charge being £1 per Car above the ordinary rates, which are 9s. for cars not exceeding half-a-ton, and 14s. for cars above 10 cwts., including wharfage and porterage at Lymington and Yarmouth.

BANK HOLIDAYS ARE TREATED AS ORDINARY WEEK-DAYS; GOOD FRIDAY AND CHRISTMAS DAY AS SUNDAYS,

Unloading Motor Cars at Yarmouth, I. of W.

Acknowledgements

No book like this can be written without a great deal of help from others and this the authors most gratefully acknowledge. First our thanks are due to the help and advice of former Assistants in the Isle of Wight, Mr C. N. Anderson, Mr G. H. R. Gardener and Mr Gordon Nicholson, Mr I. C. M. Marshall of British Railways also. Mr I. Davis, the Locomotive Foreman at Ryde in the last months of steam was also most helpful.

Mr Scholes, the Curator of Historical Relics and Mr Cogger of the British Transport Museum and Mr E. Atkinson, the Archivist of the British Transport Historical Records have gone out of their way to put material—photographs, handbills and other matter—at our disposal.

British Railways too have kindly consented to our publication of the gradient profiles, curves and other relevant matter for all the Island lines.

Dr J. Mackett, Mr A. Blackburn, Mr R. C. Riley, Mr C. G. Woodnutt and Mr Timothy Cooper have helped us greatly with advice and information in addition to photographs. So too have Mr Green, the Seely Librarian at Newport, the Curator of the Carisbrooke Museum, Mr J. D. Jones, and the County Archivist, Mr Earl.

Michael Robbins's book 'The Isle of Wight Railways' and Messrs Blackburn and Macketts' new book on the Freshwater, Yarmouth and Newport Railway were invaluable and of course the many articles in the *Locomotive, Railway Magazine, Trains Illustrated, Railway World,* the Isle of Wight County Press and in numerous other publications. Mr Patterson Rutherford has made available to us an old London and South Western illustration of contemporary motor car transport. For information on ships we are indebted to numerous publications and works of reference.

We have been especially lucky with photographs which have reached us in great numbers, many of them of such quality that we have had the hard problem of what to leave out rather than what to include.

Finally, our thanks go to Mr Hamilton Ellis for putting aside other work in order to finish his notable picture of Newport station in time for publication.

The photographic acknowledgements are:

National Railway Museum: 1, 2, 16, 44, 45, 53, 59, 66a, 72, 105, 106, 113, 123, 124.
Author's collection: 10, 14, 22, 24, 25, 27, 29, 30, 31, 33, 34, 37, 38, 47, 54, 55, 56, 115, 116, 117.
O. J. Morris/Lens of Sutton: 4, 5, 7, 9, 42, 48, 49, 52, 57, 59, 60, 107, 109, 110, 118, 119.
Lens of Sutton: 23, 28, 39, 41, 43.
Dr J. Mackett collection: 17, 61, 75, 88, 97, 99, 100, 101, 120, 125, 127.
T. P. Cooper collection: 8, 35, 62, 63.
R. A. Silsbury collection: 11, 12, 21, 65.
R. C. Riley collection: 6, 13, 18, 19, 67, 73, 91.
LCGB/Ken Nunn collection: 15, 20.
L&GRP/David & Charles: 3, 26.

Acknowledgements

Real Photographs/Ian Allan Ltd: 19, 32, 36, 40, 50, 51, 108.
W. G. Boyden: 46.
S. W. Baker: 64, 70, 111.
G. L. Nicholson: 66.
Aerofilms Ltd: 68.
B. T. Docks Board: 69.
C. Hamilton Ellis: 71.
M. Dunnett: 74, 79, 80, 83, 86, 87, 94.
M. V. Edwards: 76, 85.
K. L. Cook: 77, 78.
G. F. Bloxam: 81.
S. R. Law: 84.
A. E. Bennett: 82, 90, 92, 93.
John Goss: 89, 102, 104, 105.
B. Stephenson: 95, 103.
N. Paterson: 96.
S. C. Nash: 98.
H. F. Wheeller: 112, 114.
H. C. Casserley: 121.
C. G. Woodnutt: 35, 122, 126.